Val d'Ar

Ten Lectures on the Tuscan Art Directly Antecedent
to the Florentine Year of Victories; Given Before the
University of Oxford in Michaelmas Term, 1873

John Ruskin

Alpha Editions

This edition published in 2024

ISBN : 9789362096142

Design and Setting By
Alpha Editions
www.alphaedis.com
Email - info@alphaedis.com

Contents

LECTURE I.
NICHOLAS THE PISAN.

1. On this day, of this month, the 20th of October, six hundred and twenty-three years ago, the merchants and tradesmen of Florence met before the church of Santa Croce; marched through the city to the palace of their Podesta; deposed their Podesta; set over themselves, in his place, a knight belonging to an inferior city; called him "Captain of the People;" appointed under him a Signory of twelve Ancients chosen from among themselves; hung a bell for him on the tower of the Lion, that he might ring it at need, and gave him the flag of Florence to bear, half white, and half red.

The first blow struck upon the bell in that tower of the Lion began the tolling for the passing away of the feudal system, and began the joy-peal, or carillon, for whatever deserves joy, in that of our modern liberties, whether of action or of trade.

2. Within the space of our Oxford term from that day, namely, on the 13th of December in the same year, 1250, died, at Ferentino, in Apulia, the second Frederick, Emperor of Germany; the second also of the two great lights which in his lifetime, according to Dante's astronomy, ruled the world,—whose light being quenched, "the land which was once the residence of courtesy and valour, became the haunt of all men who are ashamed to be near the good, or to speak to them."

> *"In sul paese chadice e po riga*
>
> *solea valore e cortesia trovar si*
>
> *prima che federigo Bavessi briga,*
>
> *or puo sicuramente indi passarsi*
>
> *per qualuuche lasciassi per vergogna*
>
> *di ragionar co buoni, e appressarsi."*
>
> PURO., Cant. 16.

3. The "Paese che Adice e Po riga" is of course Lombardy; and might have been enough distinguished by the name of its principal river. But Dante has an especial reason for naming the Adige. It is always by the valley of the Adige that the power of the German Caesars descends on Italy; and that battlemented bridge, which doubtless many of you remember, thrown over the Adige at Verona, was so built that the German riders might have secure and constant access to the city. In which city they had their first stronghold in Italy, aided therein by the great family of the Montecchi, Montacutes,

Mont-aigu-s, or Montagues; lords, so called, of the mountain peaks; in feud with the family of the Cappelletti,—hatted, or, more properly, scarlet-hatted, persons. And this accident of nomenclature, assisted by your present familiar knowledge of the real contests of the sharp mountains with the flat caps, or petasoi, of cloud, (locally giving Mont Pilate its title, "Pileatus,") may in many points curiously illustrate for you that contest of Frederick the Second with Innocent the Fourth, which in the good of it and the evil alike, represents to all time the war of the solid, rational, and earthly authority of the King, and State, with the more or less spectral, hooded, imaginative, and nubiform authority of the Pope, and Church.

4. It will be desirable also that you clearly learn the material relations, governing spiritual ones,—as of the Alps to their clouds, so of the plains to their rivers. And of these rivers, chiefly note the relation to each other, first, of the Adige and Po; then of the Arno and Tiber. For the Adige, representing among the rivers and fountains of waters the channel of Imperial, as the Tiber of the Papal power, and the strength of the Coronet being founded on the white peaks that look down upon Hapsburg and Hohenzollern, as that of the Scarlet Cap in the marsh of the Campagna, "quo tenuis in sicco aqua destituisset," the study of the policies and arts of the cities founded in the two great valleys of Lombardy and Tuscany, so far as they were affected by their bias to the Emperor, or the Church, will arrange itself in your minds at once in a symmetry as clear as it will be, in our future work, secure and suggestive.

5. "Tenuis, in sicco." How literally the words apply, as to the native streams, so to the early states or establishings of the great cities of the world. And you will find that the policy of the Coronet, with its tower-building; the policy of the Hood, with its dome-building; and the policy of the bare brow, with its cot-building,—the three main associations of human energy to which we owe the architecture of our earth, (in contradistinction to the dens and caves of it,)—are curiously and eternally governed by mental laws, corresponding to the physical ones which are ordained for the rocks, the clouds, and the streams.

The tower, which many of you so well remember the daily sight of, in your youth, above the "winding shore" of Thames,—the tower upon the hill of London; the dome which still rises above its foul and terrestrial clouds; and the walls of this city itself, which has been "alma," nourishing in gentleness, to the youth of England, because defended from external hostility by the difficultly fordable streams of its plain, may perhaps, in a few years more, be swept away as heaps of useless stone; but the rocks, and clouds, and rivers of our country will yet, one day, restore to it the glory of law, of religion, and of life.

6. I am about to ask you to read the hieroglyphs upon the architecture of a dead nation, in character greatly resembling our own,—in laws and in commerce greatly influencing our own;—in arts, still, from her grave, tutress of the present world. I know that it will be expected of me to explain the merits of her arts, without reference to the wisdom of her laws; and to describe the results of both, without investigating the feelings which regulated either. I cannot do this; but I will at once end these necessarily vague, and perhaps premature, generalizations; and only ask you to study some portions of the life and work of two men, father and son, citizens of the city in which the energies of this great people were at first concentrated; and to deduce from that study the conclusions, or follow out the inquiries, which it may naturally suggest.

7. It is the modern fashion to despise Vasari. He is indeed despicable, whether as historian or critic,—not least in his admiration of Michael Angelo; nevertheless, he records the traditions and opinions of his day; and these you must accurately know, before you can wisely correct. I will take leave, therefore, to begin to-day with a sentence from Vasari, which many of you have often heard quoted, but of which, perhaps, few have enough observed the value.

"Niccola Pisano finding himself under certain Greek sculptors who were carving the figures and other intaglio ornaments of the cathedral of Pisa, and of the temple of St. John, and there being, among many spoils of marbles, brought by the Pisan fleet, {1} some ancient tombs, there was one among the others most fair, on which was sculptured the hunting of Meleager." {2}

{Footnote 1: "Armata." The proper word for a land army is "esercito."}

{Footnote 2: Vol. i., p. 60, of Mrs. Foster's English translation, to which I shall always refer, in order that English students may compare the context if they wish. But the pieces of English which I give are my own direct translation, varying, it will be found, often, from Mrs. Foster's, in minute, but not unimportant, particulars.}

Get the meaning and contents of this passage well into your minds. In the gist of it, it is true, and very notable.

8. You are in mid thirteenth century; 1200-1300. The Greek nation has been dead in heart upwards of a thousand years; its religion dead, for six hundred. But through the wreck of its faith, and death in its heart, the skill of its hands, and the cunning of its design, instinctively linger. In the centuries of Christian power, the Christians are still unable to build but under Greek masters, and by pillage of Greek shrines; and their best workman is only an apprentice to the 'Graeculi esurientes' who are carving the temple of St. John.

9. Think of it. Here has the New Testament been declared for 1200 years. No spirit of wisdom, as yet, has been given to its workmen, except that which has descended from the Mars Hill on which St. Paul stood contemptuous in pity. No Bezaleel arises, to build new tabernacles, unless he has been taught by Daedalus.

10. It is necessary, therefore, for you first to know precisely the manner of these Greek masters in their decayed power; the manner which Vasari calls, only a sentence before, "That old Greek manner, blundering, disproportioned,"—Goffa, e sproporzionata.

"Goffa," the very word which Michael Angelo uses of Perugino. Behold, the Christians despising the Dunce Greeks, as the Infidel modernists despise the Dunce Christians. {1}

{Footnote 1: Compare "Ariadne Floreutina," § 46.}

11. I sketched for you, when I was last at Pisa, a few arches of the apse of the duomo, and a small portion of the sculpture of the font of the Temple of St. John. I have placed them in your rudimentary series, as examples of "quella vecchia maniera Greca, goffa e sproporzionata." My own judgment respecting them is,—and it is a judgment founded on knowledge which you may, if you choose, share with me, after working with me,—that no architecture on this grand scale, so delicately skilful in execution, or so daintily disposed in proportion, exists elsewhere in the world.

12. Is Vasari entirely wrong then?

No, only half wrong, but very fatally half wrong. There are Greeks, and Greeks.

This head with the inlaid dark iris in its eyes, from the font of St. John, is as pure as the sculpture of early Greece, a hundred years before Phidias; and it is so delicate, that having drawn with equal care this and the best work of the Lombardi at Venice (in the church of the Miracoli), I found this to possess the more subtle qualities of design. And yet, in the cloisters of St. John Lateran at Rome, you have Greek work, if not contemporary with this at Pisa, yet occupying a parallel place in the history of architecture, which is abortive, and monstrous beyond the power of any words to describe. Vasari knew no difference between these two kinds of Greek work. Nor do your modern architects. To discern the difference between the sculpture of the font of Pisa, and the spandrils of the Lateran cloister, requires thorough training of the hand in the finest methods of draughtsmanship; and, secondly, trained habit of reading the mythology and ethics of design. I simply assure you of the fact at present; and if you work, you may have sight and sense of it.

13. There are Greeks, and Greeks, then, in the twelfth century, differing as much from each other as vice, in all ages, must differ from virtue. But in Vasari's sight they are alike; in ours, they must be so, as far as regards our present purpose. As men of a school, they are to be summed under the general name of 'Byzantines;' their work all alike showing specific characters of attenuate, rigid, and in many respects offensively unbeautiful, design, to which Vasari's epithets of "goffa, e sproporzionata" are naturally applied by all persons trained only in modern principles. Under masters, then, of this Byzantine race, Niccola is working at Pisa.

14. Among the spoils brought by her fleets from Greece, is a sarcophagus, with Meleager's hunt on it, wrought "con bellissima maniera," says Vasari.

You may see that sarcophagus—any of you who go to Pisa;—touch it, for it is on a level with your hand; study it, as Niccola studied it, to your mind's content. Within ten yards of it, stand equally accessible pieces of Niccola's own work and of his son's. Within fifty yards of it, stands the Byzantine font of the chapel of St. John. Spend but the good hours of a single day quietly by these three pieces of marble, and you may learn more than in general any of you bring home from an entire tour in Italy. But how many of you ever yet went into that temple of St. John, knowing what to look for; or spent as much time in the Campo Santo of Pisa, as you do in Mr. Ryman's shop on a rainy day?

15. The sarcophagus is not, however, (with Vasari's pardon) in 'bellissima maniera' by any means. But it is in the classical Greek manner instead of the Byzantine Greek manner. You have to learn the difference between these.

Now I have explained to you sufficiently, in "Aratra Pentelici," what the classical Greek manner is. The manner and matter of it being easily summed—as those of natural and unaffected life;—nude life when nudity is right and pure; not otherwise. To Niccola, the difference between this natural Greek school, and the Byzantine, was as the difference between the bull of Thurium and of Delhi, (see Plate 19 of "Aratra Pentelici").

Instantly he followed the natural fact, and became the Father of Sculpture to Italy.

16. Are we, then, also to be strong by following the natural fact?

Yes, assuredly. That is the beginning and end of all my teaching to you. But the noble natural fact, not the ignoble. You are to study men; not lice nor entozoa. And you are to study the souls of men in their bodies, not their bodies only. Mulready's drawings from the nude are more degraded and bestial than the worst grotesques of the Byzantine or even the Indian image makers. And your modern mob of English and American tourists, following a lamplighter through the Vatican to have pink light thrown for them on the

Apollo Belvidere, are farther from capacity of understanding Greek art, than the parish charity boy, making a ghost out of a turnip, with a candle inside.

17. Niccola followed the facts, then. He is the Master of Naturalism in Italy. And I have drawn for you his lioness and cubs, to fix that in your minds. And beside it, I put the Lion of St. Mark's, that you may see exactly the kind of change he made. The Lion of St. Mark's (all but his wings, which have been made and fastened on in the fifteenth century), is in the central Byzantine manner; a fine decorative piece of work, descending in true genealogy from the Lion of Nemea, and the crested skin of him that clothes the head of the Heracles of Camarina. It has all the richness of Greek Daedal work,—nay, it has fire and life beyond much Greek Daedal work; but in so far as it is non-natural, symbolic, decorative, and not like an actual lion, it would be felt by Niccola Pisano to be imperfect. And instead of this decorative evangelical preacher of a lion, with staring eyes, and its paw on a gospel, he carves you a quite brutal and maternal lioness, with affectionate eyes, and paw set on her cub.

18. Fix that in your minds, then. Niccola Pisano is the Master of Naturalism in Italy,—therefore elsewhere; of Naturalism, and all that follows. Generally of truth, common-sense, simplicity, vitality,—and of all these, with consummate power. A man to be enquired about, is not he? and will it not make a difference to you whether you look, when you travel in Italy, in his rough early marbles for this fountain of life, or only glance at them because your Murray's Guide tells you,—and think them "odd old things"?

19. We must look for a moment more at one odd old thing—the sarcophagus which was his tutor. Upon it is carved the hunting of Meleager; and it was made, or by tradition received as, the tomb of the mother of the Countess Matilda. I must not let you pass by it without noticing two curious coincidences in these particulars. First, in the Greek subject which is given Niccola to read.

The boar, remember, is Diana's enemy. It is sent upon the fields of Calydon in punishment of the refusal of the Calydonians to sacrifice to her. 'You have refused *me*,' she said; 'you will not have Artemis Laphria, Forager Diana, to range in your fields. You shall have the Forager Swine, instead.'

Meleager and Atalanta are Diana's servants,—servants of all order, purity, due sequence of season, and time. The orbed architecture of Tuscany, with its sculptures of the succession of the labouring months, as compared with the rude vaults and monstrous imaginations of the past, was again the victory of Meleager.

20. Secondly, take what value there is in the tradition that this

sarcophagus was made the tomb of the mother of the

Countess Matilda. If you look to the fourteenth chapter of the third volume of "Modern Painters," you will find the mythic character of the Countess Matilda, as Dante employed it explained at some length. She is the representative of Natural Science as opposed to Theological.

21. Chance coincidences merely, these; but full of teaching for us, looking back upon the past. To Niccola, the piece of marble was, primarily, and perhaps exclusively, an example of free chiselling, and humanity of treatment. What else it was to him,—what the spirits of Atalanta and Matilda could bestow on him, depended on what he was himself. Of which Vasari tells you nothing. Not whether he was gentleman or clown—rich or poor—soldier or sailor. Was he never, then, in those fleets that brought the marbles back from the ravaged Isles of Greece? was he at first only a labourer's boy among the scaffoldings of the Pisan apse,—his apron loaded with dust—and no man praising him for his speech? Rough he was, assuredly; probably poor; fierce and energetic, beyond even the strain of Pisa,—just and kind, beyond the custom of his age, knowing the Judgment and Love of God: and a workman, with all his soul and strength, all his days.

22. You hear the fame of him as of a sculptor only. It is right that you should; for every great architect must be a sculptor, and be renowned, as such, more than by his building. But Niccola Pisano had even more influence on Italy as a builder than as a carver.

For Italy, at this moment, wanted builders more than carvers; and a change was passing through her life, of which external edifice was a necessary sign. I complained of you just now that you never looked at the Byzantine font in the temple of St. John. The sacristan generally will not let you. He takes you to a particular spot on the floor, and sings a musical chord. The chord returns in prolonged echo from the chapel roof, as if the building were all one sonorous marble bell.

Which indeed it is; and travellers are always greatly amused at being allowed to ring this bell; but it never occurs to them to ask how it came to be ringable:—how that tintinnabulate roof differs from the dome of the Pantheon, expands into the dome of Florence, or declines into the whispering gallery of St. Paul's.

23. When you have had full satisfaction of the tintinnabulate roof, you are led by the sacristan and Murray to Niccola Pisano's pulpit; which, if you have spare time to examine it, you find to have six sides, to be decorated with

tablets of sculpture, like the sides of the sarcophagus, and to be sustained on seven pillars, three of which are themselves carried on the backs of as many animals.

All this arrangement had been contrived before Niccola's time, and executed again and again. But behold! between the capitals of the pillars and the sculptured tablets there are interposed five cusped arches, the hollow beneath the pulpit showing dark through their foils. You have seen such cusped arches before, you think?

Yes, gentlemen, *you* have; but the Pisans had *not*. And that intermediate layer of the pulpit means—the change, in a word, for all Europe, from the Parthenon to Amiens Cathedral. For Italy it means the rise of her Gothic dynasty; it means the duomo of Milan instead of the temple of Paestum.

24. I say the duomo of Milan, only to put the change well before your eyes, because you all know that building so well. The duomo of Milan is of entirely bad and barbarous Gothic, but the passion of pinnacle and fret is in it, visibly to you, more than in other buildings. It will therefore serve to show best what fulness of change this pulpit of Niccola Pisano signifies.

In it there is no passion of pinnacle nor of fret. You see the edges of it, instead of being bossed, or knopped, or crocketed, are mouldings of severest line. No vaulting, no clustered shafts, no traceries, no fantasies, no perpendicular flights of aspiration. Steady pillars, each of one polished block; useful capitals, one trefoiled arch between them; your panel above it; thereon your story of the founder of Christianity. The whole standing upon beasts, they being indeed the foundation of us, (which Niccola knew far better than Mr. Darwin); Eagle to carry your Gospel message—Dove you think it ought to be?

{Illustration: PLATE II.—NICCOLA PISANO'S PULPIT.}

Eagle, says Niccola, and not as symbol of St. John Evangelist only, but behold! with prey between its claws. For the Gospel, it is Niccola's opinion, is not altogether a message that you may do whatever you like, and go straight to heaven. Finally, a slab of marble, cut hollow a little to bear your book; space enough for you to speak from at ease,—and here is your first architecture of Gothic Christianity!

25. Indignant thunder of dissent from German doctors,—clamour from French savants. 'What! and our Treves, and our Strasburg, and our Poictiers, and our Chartres! And you call *this* thing the first architecture of Christianity!' Yes, my French and German friends, very fine the buildings you have mentioned are; and I am bold to say I love them far better than you do, for you will run a railroad through any of them any day that you can turn a penny by it. I thank you also, Germans, in the name of our Lady of Strasburg, for

your bullets and fire; and I thank you, Frenchmen, in the name of our Lady of Rouen, for your new haberdashers' shops in the Gothic town;— meanwhile have patience with me a little, and let me go on.

26. No passion of fretwork, or pinnacle whatever, I said, is in this Pisan pulpit. The trefoiled arch itself, pleasant as it is, seems forced a little; out of perfect harmony with the rest (see Plate II.). Unnatural, perhaps, to Niccola?

Altogether unnatural to him, it is; such a thing never would have come into his head, unless some one had shown it him. Once got into his head, he puts it to good use; perhaps even he will let this somebody else put pinnacles and crockets into his head, or at least, into his son's, in a little while. Pinnacles,— crockets,—it may be, even traceries. The ground-tier of the baptistery is round-arched, and has no pinnacles; but look at its first story. The clerestory of the Duomo of Pisa has no traceries, but look at the cloister of its Campo Santo.

27. I pause at the words;—for they introduce a new group of thoughts, which presently we must trace farther.

The Holy Field;—field of burial. The "cave of Machpelah which is before Mamre," of the Pisans. "There they buried Abraham, and Sarah his wife; there they buried Isaac, and Rebekah his wife; and there I buried Leah."

How do you think such a field becomes holy,—how separated, as the resting-place of loving kindred, from that other field of blood, bought to bury strangers in?

When you have finally succeeded, by your gospel of mammon, in making all the men of your own nation not only strangers to each other, but enemies; and when your every churchyard becomes therefore a field of the stranger, the kneeling hamlet will vainly drink the chalice of God in the midst of them. The field will be unholy. No cloisters of noble history can ever be built round such an one.

28. But the very earth of this at Pisa was holy, as you know. That "armata" of the Tuscan city brought home not only marble and ivory, for treasure; but earth,—a fleet's burden,—from the place where there was healing of soul's leprosy: and their field became a place of holy tombs, prepared for its office with earth from the land made holy by one tomb; which all the knighthood of Christendom had been pouring out its life to win.

29. I told you just now that this sculpture of Niccola's was the beginning of Christian architecture. How do you judge that Christian architecture in the deepest meaning of it to differ from all other?

All other noble architecture is for the glory of living gods and men; but this is for the glory of death, in God and man. Cathedral, cloister, or tomb,—

shrine for the body of Christ, or for the bodies of the saints. All alike signifying death to this world;—life, other than of this world.

Observe, I am not saying how far this feeling, be it faith, or be it imagination, is true or false;—I only desire you to note that the power of all Christian work begins in the niche of the catacomb and depth of the sarcophagus, and is to the end definable as architecture of the tomb.

30. Not altogether, and under every condition, sanctioned in doing such honour to the dead by the Master of it. Not every grave is by His command to be worshipped. Graves there may be—too little guarded, yet dishonourable;—"ye are as graves that appear not, and the men that walk over them are not aware of them." And graves too much guarded, yet dishonourable, "which indeed appear beautiful outwardly, but are within full of all uncleanness." Or graves, themselves honourable, yet which it may be, in us, a crime to adorn. "For they indeed killed them, and ye build their sepulchres."

Questions, these, collateral; or to be examined in due time; for the present it is enough for us to know that all Christian architecture, as such, has been hitherto essentially of tombs.

It has been thought, gentlemen, that there is a fine Gothic revival in your streets of Oxford, because you have a Gothic door to your County Bank:

Remember, at all events, it was other kind of buried treasure, and bearing other interest, which Niccola Pisano's Gothic was set to guard.

LECTURE II.
JOHN THE PISAN.

31. I closed my last lecture with the statement, on which I desired to give you time for reflection, that Christian architecture was, in its chief energy, the adornment of tombs,—having the passionate function of doing honour to the dead.

But there is an ethic, or simply didactic and instructive architecture, the decoration of which you will find to be normally representative of the virtues which are common alike to Christian and Greek. And there is a natural tendency to adopt such decoration, and the modes of design fitted for it, in civil buildings. {1}

{Footnote: "These several rooms were indicated by symbol and device: Victory for the soldier, Hope for the exile, the Muses for the poets, Mercury for the artists, Paradise for the preacher."—(Sagacius Gazata, of the Palace of Can Grande. I translate only Sismondi's quotation.)}

32. *Civil*, or *civic*, I say, as opposed to military. But again observe, there are two kinds of military building. One, the robber's castle, or stronghold, out of which he issues to pillage; the other, the honest man's castle, or stronghold, into which he retreats from pillage. They are much like each other in external forms;—but Injustice, or Unrighteousness, sits in the gate of the one, veiled with forest branches, (see Giotto's painting of him); and Justice or Righteousness *enters* by the gate of the other, over strewn forest branches. Now, for example of this second kind of military architecture, look at Carlyle's account of Henry the Fowler, {1} and of his building military towns, or burgs, to protect his peasantry. In such function you have the first and proper idea of a walled town,—a place into which the pacific country people can retire for safety, as the Athenians in the Spartan war. Your fortress of this kind is a religious and civil fortress, or burg, defended by burgers, trained to defensive war. Keep always this idea of the proper nature of a fortified city:—Its walls mean protection,—its gates hospitality and triumph. In the language familiar to you, spoken of the chief of cities: "Its walls are to be Salvation, and its gates to be Praise." And recollect always the inscription over the north gate of Siena: "Cor magis tibi Sena pandit."—"More than her gates, Siena opens her heart to you."

{Footnote 1: "Frederick," vol. i.}

33. When next you enter London by any of the great lines, I should like you to consider, as you approach the city, what the feelings of the heart of London are likely to be on your approach, and at what part of the railroad station an inscription, explaining such state of her heart, might be most fitly

inscribed. Or you would still better understand the difference between ancient and modern principles of architecture by taking a cab to the Elephant and Castle, and thence walking to London Bridge by what is in fact the great southern entrance of London. The only gate receiving you is, however, the arch thrown over the road to carry the South-Eastern Railway itself; and the only exhibition either of Salvation or Praise is in the cheap clothes' shops on each side; and especially in one colossal haberdasher's shop, over which you may see the British flag waving (in imitation of Windsor Castle) when the master of the shop is at home. 34. Next to protection from external hostility, the two necessities in a city are of food and water supply;—the latter essentially constant. You can store food and forage, but water must flow freely. Hence the Fountain and the Mercato become the centres of civil architecture.

Premising thus much, I will ask you to look once more at this cloister of the Campo Santo of Pisa.

35. On first entering the place, its quiet, its solemnity, the perspective of its aisles, and the conspicuous grace and precision of its traceries, combine to give you the sensation of having entered a true Gothic cloister. And if you walk round it hastily, and, glancing only at a fresco or two, and the confused tombs erected against them, return to the uncloistered sunlight of the piazza, you may quite easily carry away with you, and ever afterwards retain, the notion that the Campo Santo of Pisa is the same kind of thing as the cloister of Westminster Abbey.

36. I will beg you to look at the building, thus photographed, more attentively. The "long-drawn aisle" is here, indeed,—but where is the "fretted vault"?

A timber roof, simple as that of a country barn, and of which only the horizontal beams catch the eye, connects an entirely plain outside wall with an interior one, pierced by round-headed openings; in which are inserted pieces of complex tracery, as foreign in conception to the rest of the work as if the Pisan armata had gone up the Rhine instead of to Crete, pillaged South Germany, and cut these pieces of tracery out of the windows of some church in an advanced stage of fantastic design at Nuremberg or Frankfort.

37. If you begin to question, hereupon, who was the Italian robber, whether of marble or thought, and look to your Vasari, you find the building attributed to John the Pisan; {1}—and you suppose the son to have been so pleased by his father's adoption of Gothic forms that he must needs borrow them, in this manner, ready made, from the Germans, and thrust them into his round arches, or wherever else they would go.

{Footnote 1: The present traceries are of fifteenth century work, founded on Giovanni's design.}

We will look at something more of his work, however, before drawing such conclusion.

38. In the centres of the great squares of Siena and Perugia, rose, obedient to engineers' art, two perennial fountains Without engineers' art, the glens which cleave the sand-rock of Siena flow with living water; and still, if there be a hell for the forger in Italy, he remembers therein the sweet grotto and green wave of Fonte Branda. But on the very summit of the two hills, crested by their great civic fortresses, and in the centres of their circuit of walls, rose the two guided wells; each in basin of goodly marble, sculptured—at Perugia, by John of Pisa, at Siena, by James of Quercia.

39. It is one of the bitterest regrets of my life (and I have many which some men would find difficult to bear,) that I never saw, except when I was a youth, and then with sealed eyes, Jacopo della Quercia's fountain. {1} The Sienese, a little while since, tore it down, and put up a model of it by a modern carver. In like manner, perhaps, you will some day knock the Elgin marbles to pieces, and commission an Academician to put up new ones,—the Sienese doing worse than that (as if the Athenians were *themselves* to break their Phidias' work).

{Footnote 1: I observe that Charles Dickens had the fortune denied to me. "The market-place, or great Piazza, is a large square, with a great broken-nosed fountain in it." ("Pictures from Italy.")}

But the fountain of John of Pisa, though much injured, and glued together with asphalt, is still in its place.

40. I will now read to you what Vasari first says of him, and it. (I. 67.) "Nicholas had, among other sons, one called John, who, because he always followed his father, and, under his discipline, intended (bent himself to, with a will,) sculpture and architecture, in a few years became not only equal to his father, but in some things superior to him; wherefore Nicholas, being now old, retired himself into Pisa, and living quietly there, left the government of everything to his son. Accordingly, when Pope Urban IV. died in Perugia, sending was made for John, who, going there, made the tomb of that Pope of marble, the which, together with that of Pope Martin IV., was afterwards thrown down, when the Perugians

{Illustration: PLATE III.—THE FOUNTAIN OF PERUGIA.}

enlarged their vescovado; so that only a few relics are seen sprinkled about the church. And the Perugians, having at the same time brought from the mountain of Pacciano, two miles distant from the city, through canals of lead, a most abundant water, by means of the invention and industry of a friar of the order of St. Silvester, it was given to John the Pisan to make all the ornaments of this fountain, as well of bronze as of marble. On which he set hand to it, and made there three orders of vases, two of marble and one of bronze. The first is put upon twelve degrees of twelve-faced steps; the second is upon some columns which put it upon a level with the first one;" (that is, in the middle of it,) "and the third, which is of bronze, rests upon three figures which have in the middle of them some griffins, of bronze too, which pour water out on every side."

41. Many things we have to note in this passage, but first I will show you the best picture I can of the thing itself.

The best I can; the thing itself being half destroyed, and what remains so beautiful that no one can now quite rightly draw it; but Mr. Arthur Severn, (the son of Keats's Mr. Severn,) was with me, looking reverently at those remains, last summer, and has made, with help from the sun, this sketch for you (Plate III.); entirely true and effective as far as his time allowed.

Half destroyed, or more, I said it was,—Time doing grievous work on it, and men worse. You heard Vasari saying of it, that it stood on twelve degrees of twelve-faced steps. These—worn, doubtless, into little more than a rugged slope—have been replaced by the moderns with four circular steps, and an iron railing; {1} the bas-reliefs have been carried off from the panels of the second vase, and its fair marble lips choked with asphalt:—of what remains, you have here a rough but true image.

{Footnote 1: In Mr. Severn's sketch, the form of the original foundation is approximately restored.}

In which you see there is not a trace of Gothic feeling or design of any sort. No crockets, no pinnacles, no foils, no vaultings, no grotesques in sculpture. Panels between pillars, panels carried on pillars, sculptures in those panels like the Metopes of the Parthenon; a Greek vase in the middle, and griffins in the middle of that. Here is your font, not at all of Saint John, but of profane and civil-engineering John. This is *his* manner of baptism of the town of Perugia.

42. Thus early, it seems, the antagonism of profane Greek to ecclesiastical Gothic declares itself. It seems as if in Perugia, as in London, you had the fountains in Trafalgar Square against Queen Elinor's Cross; or the viaduct and railway station contending with the Gothic chapel, which the master of the large manufactory close by has erected, because he thinks pinnacles and crockets have a pious influence; and will prevent his workmen from asking for shorter hours, or more wages.

43. It *seems* only; the antagonism is quite of another kind,—or, rather, of many other kinds. But note at once how complete it is—how utterly this Greek fountain of Perugia, and the round arches of Pisa, are opposed to the school of design which gave the trefoils to Niccola's pulpit, and the traceries to Giovanni's Campo Santo.

The antagonism, I say, is of another kind than ours; but deep and wide; and to explain it, I must pass for a time to apparently irrelevant topics.

You were surprised, I hope, (if you were attentive enough to catch the points in what I just now read from Vasari,) at my venturing to bring before you, just after I had been using violent language against the Sienese for breaking up the work of Quercia, that incidental sentence giving account of the much more disrespectful destruction, by the Perugians, of the tombs of Pope Urban IV., and Martin IV. Sending was made for John, you see, first, when Pope Urban IV. died in Perugia—whose tomb was to be carved by John; the Greek fountain being a secondary business. But the tomb was so well destroyed, afterwards, that only a few relics remained scattered here and there.

The tomb, I have not the least doubt, was Gothic;—and the breaking of it to pieces was not in order to restore it afterwards, that a living architect might get the job of restoration. Here is a stone out of one of Giovanni Pisano's loveliest Gothic buildings, which I myself saw with my own eyes dashed out, that a modern builder might be paid for putting in another. But Pope Urban's tomb was not destroyed to such end. There was no qualm of the belly, driving the hammer,—qualm of the conscience probably; at all events, a deeper or loftier antagonism than one on points of taste, or economy.

44. You observed that I described this Greek profane manner of design as properly belonging to *civil* buildings, as opposed not only to ecclesiastical buildings, but to military ones. Justice, or Righteousness, and Veracity, are the characters of Greek art. These *may* be opposed to religion, when religion becomes fantastic; but they *must* be opposed to war, when war becomes unjust. And if, perchance, fantastic religion and unjust war happen to go hand in hand, your Greek artist is likely to use his hammer against them spitefully enough.

45. His hammer, or his Greek fire. Hear now this example of the engineering ingenuities of our Pisan papa, in his younger days.

"The Florentines having begun, in Niccola's time, to throw down many towers, which had been built in a barbarous manner through the whole city; either that the people might be less hurt, by their means, in the fights that often took place between the Guelphs and Ghibellines, or else that there might be greater security for the State, it appeared to them that it would be very difficult to ruin the Tower of the Death-watch, which was in the place of St. John, because it had its walls built with such a grip in them that the stones could not be stirred with the pickaxe, and also because it was of the loftiest; whereupon Nicholas, causing the tower to be cut, at the foot of it, all the length of one of its sides; and closing up the cut, as he made it, with short (wooden) under-props, about a yard long, and setting fire to them, when the props were burned, the tower fell, and broke itself nearly all to pieces: which was held a thing so ingenious and so useful for such affairs, that it has since passed into a custom, so that when it is needful, in this easiest manner, any edifice may be thrown down."

46. 'When it is needful.' Yes; but when is that? If instead of the towers of the Death-watch in the city, one could ruin the towers of the Death-watch of evil pride and evil treasure in men's hearts, there would be need enough for such work both in Florence and London. But the walls of those spiritual towers have still stronger 'grip' in them, and are fireproof with a vengeance.

"Le mure me parean die ferro fosse,

. . . e el mi dixe, il fuoco eterno

Chentro laffoca, le dimostra rosse."

But the towers in Florence, shattered to fragments by this ingenious engineer, and the tombs in Perugia, which his son will carve, only that they also may be so well destroyed that only a few relics remain, scattered up and down the church,—are these, also, only the iron towers, and the red-hot tombs, of the city of Dis?

Let us see.

47. In order to understand the relation of the tradesmen and working men, including eminently the artist, to the general life of the thirteenth century, I must lay before you the clearest elementary charts I can of the course which the fates of Italy were now appointing for her.

My first chart must be geographical. I want you to have a clearly dissected and closely fitted notion of the natural boundaries of her states, and their relations to surrounding ones. Lay hold first, firmly, of your conception of the valleys of the Po and the Arno, running counter to each other—opening east and opening west,—Venice at the end of the one, Pisa at the end of the other.

48. These two valleys—the hearts of Lombardy and Etruria—virtually contain the life of Italy. They are entirely different in character: Lombardy, essentially luxurious and worldly, at this time rude in art, but active; Etruria, religious, intensely imaginative, and inheriting refined forms of art from before the days of Porsenna.

49. South of these, in mid-Italy, you have Romagna,—the valley of the Tiber. In that valley, decayed Rome, with her lust of empire inextinguishable;—no inheritance of imaginative art, nor power of it; dragging her own ruins hourly into more fantastic ruin, and defiling her faith hourly with more fantastic guilt.

South of Romagna, you have the kingdoms of Calabria and Sicily,—-Magna Graecia, and Syracuse, in decay;——strange spiritual fire from the Saracenic east still lighting the volcanic land, itself laid all in ashes.

50. Conceive Italy then always in these four masses: Lombardy, Etruria, Romagna, Calabria.

Now she has three great external powers to deal with: the western, France— the northern, Germany—the eastern, Arabia. On her right the Frank; on her left the Saracen; above her, the Teuton. And roughly, the French are a religious chivalry; the Germans a profane chivalry; the Saracens an infidel chivalry. What is best of each is benefiting Italy; what is worst, afflicting her. And in the time we are occupied with, all are afflicting her.

What Charlemagne, Barbarossa, or Saladin did to teach her, you can trace only by carefullest thought. But in this thirteenth century all these three powers are adverse to her, as to each other. Map the methods of their adversity thus:—-

51. Germany, (profane chivalry,) is vitally adverse to the Popes; endeavouring to establish imperial and knightly power against theirs. It is fiercely, but frankly, covetous of Italian territory, seizes all it can of Lombardy and Calabria, and with any help procurable either from robber Christians or robber Saracens, strives, in an awkward manner, and by open force, to make itself master of Rome, and all Italy.

52. France, all surge and foam of pious chivalry, lifts herself in fitful rage of devotion, of avarice, and of pride. She is the natural ally of the church; makes her own monks the proudest of the Popes; raises Avignon into another Rome; prays and pillages insatiably; pipes pastoral songs of innocence, and invents grotesque variations of crime; gives grace to the rudeness of England, and venom to the cunning of Italy. She is a chimera among nations, and one knows not whether to admire most the valour of Guiscard, the virtue of St. Louis or the villany of his brother.

53. The Eastern powers—Greek, Israelite, Saracen—are at once the enemies of the Western, their prey, and their tutors.

They bring them methods of ornament and of merchandise, and stimulate in them the worst conditions of pugnacity, bigotry, and rapine. That is the broad geographical and political relation of races. Next, you must consider the conditions of their time.

54. I told you, in my second lecture on Engraving, that before the twelfth century the nations were too savage to be Christian, and after the fifteenth too carnal to be Christian.

The delicacy of sensation and refinements of imagination necessary to understand Christianity belong to the mid period when men risen from a life of brutal hardship are not yet fallen to one of brutal luxury. You can neither comprehend the character of Christ while you are chopping flints for tools, and gnawing raw bones for food; nor when you have ceased to do anything with either tools or hands, and dine on gilded capons. In Dante's lines, beginning

"I saw Bellincion Berti walk abroad

In leathern girdle, with a clasp of bone,"

you have the expression of his sense of the increasing luxury of the age, already sapping its faith. But when Bellincion Berti walked abroad in skins not yet made into leather, and with the bones of his dinner in a heap at his door, instead of being cut into girdle clasps, he was just as far from capacity of being a Christian.

55. The following passage, from Carlyle's "Chartism," expresses better than any one else has done, or is likely to do it, the nature of this Christian era, (extending from the twelfth to the sixteenth century,) in England,—the like being entirely true of it elsewhere:—

"In those past silent centuries, among those silent classes, much had been going on. Not only had red deer in the New and other forests been got preserved and shot; and treacheries {1} of Simon de Montfort, wars of Red and White Roses, battles of Crecy, battles of Bosworth, and many other battles, been got transacted and adjusted; but England wholly, not without sore toil and aching bones to the millions of sires and the millions of sons of eighteen generations, had been got drained and tilled, covered with yellow harvests, beautiful and rich in possessions. The mud-wooden Caesters and Chesters had become steepled, tile-roofed, compact towns. Sheffield had taken to the manufacture of Sheffield whittles. Worstead could from wool spin yarn, and knit or weave the same into stockings or breeches for men. England had property valuable to the auctioneer; but the accumulate manufacturing, commercial, economic skill which lay impalpably warehoused in English hands and heads, what auctioneer could estimate?

{Footnote 1: Perhaps not altogether so, any more than Oliver's dear papa Carlyle. We may have to read *him* also, otherwise than the British populace have yet read, some day.}

"Hardly an Englishman to be met with but could do something; some cunninger thing than break his fellow-creature's head with battle-axes. The seven incorporated trades, with their million guild-brethren, with their hammers, their shuttles, and tools, what an army,—fit to conquer that land of England, as we say, and hold it conquered! Nay, strangest of all, the English people had acquired the faculty and habit of thinking,—even of believing; individual conscience had unfolded itself among them;— Conscience, and Intelligence its handmaid. {1} Ideas of innumerable kinds were circulating among these men; witness one Shakspeare, a wool-comber, poacher or whatever else, at Stratford, in Warwickshire, who happened to write books!—the finest human figure, as I apprehend, that Nature has hitherto seen fit to make of our widely Teutonic clay. Saxon, Norman, Celt, or Sarmat, I find no human soul so beautiful, these fifteen hundred known years;—our supreme modern European man. Him England had contrived to realize: were there not ideas?

{Footnote 1: Observe Carlyle's order of sequence. Perceptive Reason is the Handmaid of Conscience, not Conscience hers. If you resolve to do right, you will soon do wisely; but resolve only to do wisely, and you will never do right.}

"Ideas poetic and also Puritanic, that had to seek utterance in the notablest way! England had got her Shakspeare, but was now about to get her Milton and Oliver Cromwell. This, too, we will call a new expansion, hard as it might be to articulate and adjust; this, that a man could actually have a conscience for his own behoof, and not for his priest's only; that his priest, be he who he might, would henceforth have to take that fact along with him."

56. You observe, in this passage, account is given you of two things—(A) of the development of a powerful class of tradesmen and artists; and, (B) of the development of an individual conscience.

In the savage times you had simply the hunter, digger, and robber; now you have also the manufacturer and salesman. The ideas of ingenuity with the hand, of fairness in exchange, have occurred to us. We can do something now with our fingers, as well as with our fists; and if we want our neighbours' goods, we will not simply carry them off, as of old, but offer him some of ours in exchange.

57. Again; whereas before we were content to let our priests do for us all they could, by gesticulating, dressing, sacrificing, or beating of drums and blowing of trumpets; and also direct our steps in the way of life, without any doubt

on our part of their own perfect acquaintance with it,—we have now got to do something for ourselves—to think something for ourselves; and thus have arrived in straits of conscience which, so long as we endeavour to steer through them honestly, will be to us indeed a quite secure way of life, and of all living wisdom.

58. Now the centre of this new freedom of thought is in Germany; and the power of it is shown first, as I told you in my opening lecture, in the great struggle of Frederick II. with Rome. And German freedom of thought had certainly made some progress, when it had managed to reduce the Pope to disguise himself as a soldier, ride out of Rome by moonlight, and gallop his thirty-four miles to the seaside before

{Illustration: PLATE IV.—NORMAN IMAGERY.}

summer dawn. Here, clearly, is quite a new state of things for the Holy Father of Christendom to consider, during such wholesome horse-exercise.

59. Again; the refinements of new art are represented by France—centrally by St. Louis with his Sainte Chapelle. Happily, I am able to lay on your table to-day—having placed it three years ago in your educational series—a leaf of a Psalter, executed for St. Louis himself. He and his artists are scarcely out of their savage life yet, and have no notion of adorning the Psalms better than by pictures of long-necked cranes, long-eared rabbits, long-tailed lions, and red and white goblins putting their tongues out. {1} But in refinement of touch, in beauty of colour, in the human faculties of order and grace, they are long since, evidently, past the flint and bone stage,—refined enough, now,—subtle enough, now, to learn anything that is pretty and fine, whether in theology or any other matter.

{Footnote 1: I cannot go to the expense of engraving this most subtle example; but Plate IV. shows the average conditions of temper and imagination in religious ornamental work of the time.}

60. Lastly, the new principle of Exchange is represented by Lombardy and Venice, to such purpose that your Merchant and Jew of Venice, and your Lombard of Lombard Street, retain some considerable influence on your minds, even to this day.

And in the exact midst of all such transition, behold, Etruria with her Pisans—her Florentines,—receiving, resisting, and reigning over all: pillaging the Saracens of their marbles—binding the French bishops in silver chains;—shattering the towers of German tyranny into small pieces,—building with strange jewellery the belfry tower for newly-conceived Christianity;—and, in sacred picture, and sacred song, reaching the height, among nations, most passionate, and most pure.

I must close my lecture without indulging myself yet, by addition of detail; requesting you, before we next meet, to fix these general outlines in your minds, so that, without disturbing their distinctness, I may trace in the sequel the relations of Italian Art to these political and religious powers; and determine with what force of passionate sympathy, or fidelity of resigned obedience, the Pisan artists, father and son, executed the indignation of Florence and fulfilled the piety of Orvieto.

———————————

LECTURE III.
SHIELD AND APRON.

61. I laid before you, in my last lecture, first lines of the chart of Italian history in the thirteenth century, which I hope gradually to fill with colour, and enrich, to such degree as may be sufficient for all comfortable use. But I indicated, as the more special subject of our immediate study, the nascent power of liberal thought, and liberal art, over dead tradition and rude workmanship.

To-day I must ask you to examine in greater detail the exact relation of this liberal art to the illiberal elements which surrounded it.

62. You do not often hear me use that word "Liberal" in any favourable sense. I do so now, because I use it also in a very narrow and exact sense. I mean that the thirteenth century is, in Italy's year of life, her 17th of March. In the light of it, she assumes her toga virilis; and it is sacred to her god Liber.

63. To her god *Liber*,—observe: not Dionusos, still less Bacchus, but her own ancient and simple deity. And if you have read with some care the statement I gave you, with Carlyle's help, of the moment and manner of her change from savageness to dexterity, and from rudeness to refinement of life, you will hear, familiar as the lines are to you, the invocation in the first Georgic with a new sense of its meaning:—

"Vos, O clarissima mundi

Lumina, labentem coelo quae ducitis annum,

Liber, et alma Ceres; vestro si munere tellus

Chaoniam pingui glandem mutavit arista,

Poculaqu' inventis Acheloia miscuit uvis,

Munera vestra cano."

These gifts, innocent, rich, full of life, exquisitely beautiful in order and grace of growth, I have thought best to symbolize to you, in the series of types of the power of the Greek gods, placed in your educational series, by the blossom of the wild strawberry; which in rising from its trine cluster of trine leaves,—itself as beautiful as a white rose, and always single on its stalk, like an ear of corn, yet with a succeeding blossom at its side, and bearing a fruit which is as distinctly a group of seeds as an ear of corn itself, and yet is the pleasantest to taste of all the pleasant things prepared by nature for the food of men, {1}—may accurately symbolize, and help you to remember, the conditions of this liberal and delightful, yet entirely modest and orderly, art, and thought.

{Footnote 1: I am sorry to pack my sentences together in this confused way. But I have much to say; and cannot always stop to polish or adjust it as I used to do.}

64. You will find in the fourth of my inaugural lectures, at the 98th paragraph, this statement,—much denied by modern artists and authors, but nevertheless quite unexceptionally true,—that the entire vitality of art depends upon its having for object either to *state a true thing*, or *adorn a serviceable one*. The two functions of art in Italy, in this entirely liberal and virescent phase of it,—virgin art, we may call it, retaining the most literal sense of the words virga and virgo,—are to manifest the doctrines of a religion which now, for the first time, men had soul enough to understand; and to adorn edifices or dress, with which the completed politeness of daily life might be invested, its convenience completed, and its decorous and honourable pride satisfied.

65. That pride was, among the men who gave its character to the century, in honourableness of private conduct, and useful magnificence of public art. Not of private or domestic art: observe this very particularly.

"Such was the simplicity of private manners,"—(I am now quoting Sismondi, but with the fullest ratification that my knowledge enables me to give,)— "and the economy of the richest citizens, that if a city enjoyed repose only for a few years, it doubled its revenues, and found itself, in a sort, encumbered with its riches. The Pisans knew neither of the luxury of the table, nor that of furniture, nor that of a number of servants; yet they were sovereigns of the whole of Sardinia, Corsica, and Elba, had colonies at St. Jean d'Acre and Constantinople, and their merchants in those cities carried on the most extended commerce with the Saracens and Greeks." {1}

{Footnote 1: Sismondi; French translation, Brussels, 1838; vol. ii., p. 275.}

66. "And in that time," (I now give you my own translation of Giovanni Villani,) "the citizens of Florence lived sober, and on coarse meats, and at little cost; and had many customs and playfulnesses which were blunt and rude; and they dressed themselves and their wives with coarse cloth; many wore merely skins, with no lining, and *all* had only leathern buskins; {1} and the Florentine ladies, plain shoes and stockings with no ornaments; and the best of them were content with a close gown of coarse scarlet of Cyprus, or camlet girded with an old-fashioned clasp-girdle; and a mantle over all, lined with vaire, with a hood above; and that, they threw over their heads. The women of lower rank were dressed in the same manner, with coarse green Cambray cloth; fifty pounds was the ordinary bride's dowry, and a hundred or a hundred and fifty would in those times have been held brilliant, ('isfolgorata,' dazzling, with sense of dissipation or extravagance;) and most maidens were twenty or more before they married. Of such gross customs

were then the Florentines; but of good faith, and loyal among themselves and in their state; and in their coarse life, and poverty, did more and braver things than are done in our days with more refinement and riches."

{Footnote 1: I find this note for expansion on the margin of my lecture, but had no time to work it out:—'This lower class should be either barefoot, or have strong shoes—wooden clogs good. Pretty Boulogne sabot with purple stockings. Waterloo Road—little girl with her hair in curlpapers,—a coral necklace round her neck—the neck bare—and her boots of thin stuff, worn out, with her toes coming through, and rags hanging from her heels,—a profoundly accurate type of English national and political life. Your hair in curlpapers—borrowing tongs from every foreign nation, to pinch you into manners. The rich ostentatiously wearing coral about the bare neck; and the poor—cold as the stones and indecent.'}

67. I detain you a moment at the words "scarlet of Cyprus, or camlet."

Observe that camelot (camelet) from *kamaelotae*, camel's skin, is a stuff made of silk and camel's hair originally, afterwards of silk and wool. At Florence, the camel's hair would always have reference to the Baptist, who, as you know, in Lippi's picture, wears the camel's skin itself, made into a Florentine dress, such as Villani has just described, "col tassello sopra," with the hood above. Do you see how important the word "Capulet" is becoming to us, in its main idea?

68. Not in private nor domestic art, therefore, I repeat to you, but in useful magnificence of public art, these citizens expressed their pride:—and that public art divided itself into two branches—civil, occupied upon ethic subjects of sculpture and painting; and religious, occupied upon scriptural or traditional histories, in treatment of which, nevertheless, the nascent power and liberality of thought were apparent, not only in continual amplification and illustration of scriptural story by the artist's own invention, but in the acceptance of profane mythology, as part of the Scripture, or tradition, given by Divine inspiration.

69. Nevertheless, for the provision of things necessary in domestic life, there developed itself, together with the group of inventive artists exercising these nobler functions, a vast body of craftsmen, and, literally, *manu*facturers, workers by hand, who associated themselves, as chance, tradition, or the accessibility of material directed, in towns which thenceforward occupied a leading position in commerce, as producers of a staple of excellent, or perhaps inimitable, quality; and the linen or cambric of Cambray, the lace of Mechlin, the wool of Worstead, and the steel of Milan, implied the tranquil and hereditary skill of multitudes, living in wealthy industry, and humble honour.

70. Among these artisans, the weaver, the ironsmith, the goldsmith, the carpenter, and the mason necessarily took the principal rank, and on their occupations the more refined arts were wholesomely based, so that the five businesses may be more completely expressed thus:

The weaver and embroiderer,

The ironsmith and armourer,

The goldsmith and jeweller,

The carpenter and engineer,

The stonecutter and painter.

You have only once to turn over the leaves of Lionardo's sketch book, in the Ambrosian Library, to see how carpentry is connected with engineering,— the architect was always a stonecutter, and the stonecutter not often practically separate, as yet, from the painter, and never so in general conception of function. You recollect, at a much later period, Kent's description of Cornwall's steward:

"KENT. You cowardly rascal!—nature disclaims in thee, a tailor made thee!

CORNWALL. Thou art a strange fellow—a tailor make a man?

KENT. Ay, sir; a stonecutter, or a painter, could not have made him so ill; though they had been but two hours at the trade."

71. You may consider then this group of artizans with the merchants, as now forming in each town an important Tiers Etat, or Third State of the people, occupied in service, first, of the ecclesiastics, who in monastic bodies inhabited the cloisters round each church; and, secondly, of the knights, who, with their retainers, occupied, each family their own fort, in allied defence of their appertaining streets.

72. A Third Estate, indeed; but adverse alike to both the others, to Montague as to Capulet, when they become disturbers of the public peace; and having a pride of its own,—hereditary still, but consisting in the inheritance of skill and knowledge rather than of blood,—which expressed the sense of such inheritance by taking its name habitually from the master rather than the sire; and which, in its natural antagonism to dignities won only by violence, or recorded only by heraldry, you may think of generally as the race whose bearing is the Apron, instead of the shield.

73. When, however, these two, or in perfect subdivision three, bodies of men, lived in harmony,—the knights remaining true to the State, the clergy to their faith, and the workmen to their craft,—conditions of national force were arrived at, under which all the great art of the middle ages was accomplished.

The pride of the knights, the avarice of the priests, and the gradual abasement of character in the craftsman, changing him from a citizen able to wield either tools in peace or weapons in war, to a dull tradesman, forced to pay mercenary troops to defend his shop door, are the direct causes of common ruin towards the close of the sixteenth century.

74. But the deep underlying cause of the decline in national character itself, was the exhaustion of the Christian faith. None of its practical claims were avouched either by reason or experience; and the imagination grew weary of sustaining them in despite of both. Men could not, as their powers of reflection became developed, steadily conceive that the sins of a life might be done away with, by finishing it with Mary's name on the lips; nor could tradition of miracle for ever resist the personal discovery, made by each rude disciple by himself, that he might pray to all the saints for a twelvemonth together, and yet not get what he asked for.

75. The Reformation succeeded in proclaiming that existing Christianity was a lie; but substituted no theory of it which could be more rationally or credibly sustained; and ever since, the religion of educated persons throughout Europe has been dishonest or ineffectual; it is only among the labouring peasantry that the grace of a pure Catholicism, and the patient simplicities of the Puritan, maintain their imaginative dignity, or assert their practical use.

76. The existence of the nobler arts, however, involves the harmonious life and vital faith of the three classes whom we have just distinguished; and that condition exists, more or less disturbed, indeed, by the vices inherent in each class, yet, on the whole, energetically and productively, during the twelfth, thirteenth, fourteenth, and fifteenth centuries. But our present subject being Architecture only, I will limit your attention altogether to the state of society in the great age of architecture, the thirteenth century. A great age in all ways; but most notably so in the correspondence it presented, up to a just and honourable point, with the utilitarian energy of our own days.

77. The increase of wealth, the safety of industry, and the conception of more convenient furniture of life, to which we must attribute the rise of the entire artist class, were accompanied, in that century, by much enlargement in the conception of useful public works: and—not by *private* enterprise,—that idle persons might get dividends out of the public pocket,—but by *public* enterprise,—each citizen paying down at once his share of what was necessary to accomplish the benefit to the State,—great architectural and engineering efforts were made for the common service. Common, observe; but not, in our present sense, republican. One of the most ludicrous sentences ever written in the blindness of party spirit is that of Sismondi, in which he declares, thinking of these public works only, that 'the architecture of the thirteenth century is entirely republican.' The architecture of the

thirteenth century is, in the mass of it, simply baronial or ecclesiastical; it is of castles, palaces, or churches; but it is true that splendid civic works were also accomplished by the vigour of the newly risen popular power.

"The canal named Naviglio Graude, which brings the waters of the Ticino to Milan, traversing a distance of thirty miles, was undertaken in 1179, recommended in 1257, and, soon after, happily terminated; in it still consists the wealth of a vast extent of Lombardy. At the same time the town of Milan rebuilt its walls, which were three miles round, and had sixteen marble gates, of magnificence which might have graced the capital of all Italy. The Genovese, in 1276 and 1283, built their two splendid docks, and the great wall of their quay; and in 1295 finished the noble aqueduct which brings pure and abundant waters to their city from a great distance among their mountains. There is not a single town in Italy which at the same time did not undertake works of this kind; and while these larger undertakings were in progress, stone bridges were built across the rivers, the streets and piazzas were paved with large slabs of stone, and every free government recognized the duty of providing for the convenience of the citizens." {1}

{Footnote 1: Simondi, vol ii. chap. 10.}

78. The necessary consequence of this enthusiasm in useful building, was the formation of a vast body of craftsmen and architects; corresponding in importance to that which the railway, with its associated industry, has developed in modern times, but entirely different in personal character, and relation to the body politic.

Their personal character was founded on the accurate knowledge of their business in all respects; the ease and pleasure of unaffected invention; and the true sense of power to do everything better than it had ever been yet done, coupled with general contentment in life, and in its vigour and skill.

It is impossible to overrate the difference between such a condition of mind, and that of the modern artist, who either does not know his business at all, or knows it only to recognize his own inferiority to every former workman of distinction.

79. Again: the political relation of these artificers to the State was that of a caste entirely separate from the noblesse; {1} paid for their daily work what was just, and competing with each other to supply the best article they could for the money. And it is, again, impossible to overrate the difference between such a social condition, and that of the artists of to-day, struggling to occupy a position of equality in wealth with the noblesse,—paid irregular and monstrous prices by an entirely ignorant and selfish public; and competing with each other to supply the worst article they can for the money.

{Footnote 1: The giving of knighthood to Jacopo della Quercia for his lifelong service to Siena was not the elevation of a dexterous workman, but grace to a faithful citizen.}

I never saw anything so impudent on the walls of any exhibition, in any country, as last year in London. It was a daub professing to be a "harmony in pink and white" (or some such nonsense;) absolute rubbish, and which had taken about a quarter of an hour to scrawl or daub—it had no pretence to be called painting. The price asked for it was two hundred and fifty guineas.

80. In order to complete your broad view of the elements of social power in the thirteenth century, you have now farther to understand the position of the country people, who maintained by their labour these three classes, whose action you can discern, and whose history you can read; while, of those who maintained them, there is no history, except of the annual ravage of their fields by contending cities or nobles;—and, finally, that of the higher body of merchants, whose influence was already beginning to counterpoise the prestige of noblesse in Florence, and who themselves constituted no small portion of the noblesse of Venice.

The food-producing country was for the most part still possessed by the nobles; some by the ecclesiastics; but a portion, I do not know how large, was in the hands of peasant proprietors, of whom Sismondi gives this, to my mind, completely pleasant and satisfactory, though, to his, very painful, account:—

"They took no interest in public affairs; they had assemblies of their commune at the village in which the church of their parish was situated, and to which they retreated to defend themselves in case of war; they had also magistrates of their own choice; but all their interests appeared to them enclosed in the circle of their own commonality; they did not meddle with general politics, and held it for their point of honour to remain faithful, through all revolutions, to the State of which they formed a part, obeying, without hesitation, its chiefs, whoever they were, and by whatever title they occupied their places."

81. Of the inferior agricultural labourers, employed on the farms of the nobles and richer ecclesiastics, I find nowhere due notice, nor does any historian seriously examine their manner of life. Liable to every form of robbery and oppression, I yet regard their state as not only morally but physically happier than that of riotous soldiery, or the lower class of artizans, and as the safeguard of every civilized nation, through all its worst vicissitudes of folly and crime. Nature has mercifully appointed that seed must be sown, and sheep folded, whatever lances break, or religions fail; and at this hour, while the streets of Florence and Verona are full of idle

politicians, loud of tongue, useless of hand and treacherous of heart, there still may be seen in their market-places, standing, each by his heap of pulse or maize, the grey-haired labourers, silent, serviceable, honourable, keeping faith, untouched by change, to their country and to Heaven. {1}

{Footnote 1: Compare "Sesame and Lilies," sec. 38, p. 58. (P. 86 of the small edition of 1882.)}

82. It is extremely difficult to determine in what degree the feelings or intelligence of this class influenced the architectural design of the thirteenth century;—how far afield the cathedral tower was intended to give delight, and to what simplicity of rustic conception Quercia or Ghiberti appealed by the fascination of their Scripture history. You may at least conceive, at this date, a healthy animation in all men's minds, and the children of the vineyard and sheepcote crowding the city on its festa days, and receiving impulse to busier, if not nobler, education, in its splendour. {1}

{Footnote 1: Of detached abbeys, see note on Education of Joan of Arc, "Sesame and Lilies," sec. 82, p. 106. (P. 158 of the small edition of 1882.)}

83. The great class of the merchants is more difficult to define; but you may regard them generally as the examples of whatever modes of life might be consistent with peace and justice, in the economy of transfer, as opposed to the military license of pillage.

They represent the gradual ascendancy of foresight, prudence, and order in society, and the first ideas of advantageous national intercourse. Their body is therefore composed of the most intelligent and temperate natures of the time,—uniting themselves, not directly for the purpose of making money, but to obtain stability for equal institutions, security of property, and pacific relations with neighbouring states. Their guilds form the only representatives of true national council, unaffected, as the landed proprietors were, by merely local circumstances and accidents.

84. The strength of this order, when its own conduct was upright, and its opposition to the military body was not in avaricious cowardice, but in the resolve to compel justice and to secure peace, can only be understood by you after an examination of the great changes in the government of Florence during the thirteenth century, which, among other minor achievements interesting to us, led to that destruction of the Tower of the Death-watch, so ingeniously accomplished by Niccola Pisano. This change, and its results, will be the subject of my next lecture. I must to-day sum, and in some farther degree make clear, the facts already laid before you.

85. We have seen that the inhabitants of every great Italian state may be divided, and that very stringently, into the five classes of knights, priests, merchants, artists, and peasants. No distinction exists between artist and

artizan, except that of higher genius or better conduct; the best artist is assuredly also the best artizan; and the simplest workman uses his invention and emotion as well as his fingers. The entire body of artists is under the orders (as shopmen are under the orders of their customers), of the knights, priests, and merchants,—the knights for the most part demanding only fine goldsmiths' work, stout armour, and rude architecture; the priests commanding both the finest architecture and painting, and the richest kinds of decorative dress and jewellery,—while the merchants directed works of public use, and were the best judges of artistic skill. The competition for the Baptistery gates of Florence is before the guild of merchants; nor is their award disputed, even in thought, by any of the candidates.

86. This is surely a fact to be taken much to heart by our present communities of Liverpool and Manchester. They probably suppose, in their modesty, that lords and clergymen are the proper judges of art, and merchants can only, in the modern phrase, 'know what they like,' or follow humbly the guidance of their golden-crested or flat-capped superiors. But in the great ages of art, neither knight nor pope shows signs of true power of criticism. The artists crouch before them, or quarrel with them, according to their own tempers. To the merchants they submit silently, as to just and capable judges. And look what men these are, who submit. Donatello, Ghiberti, Quercia, Luca! If men like these submit to the merchant, who shall rebel?

87. But the still franker, and surer, judgment of innocent pleasure was awarded them by all classes alike: and the interest of the public was the *final* rule of right,—that public being always eager to see, and earnest to learn. For the stories told by their artists formed, they fully believed, a Book of Life; and every man of real genius took up his function of illustrating the scheme of human morality and salvation, as naturally, and faithfully, as an English mother of to-day giving her children their first lessons in the Bible. In this endeavour to teach they almost unawares taught themselves; the question "How shall I represent this most clearly?" became to themselves, presently, "How was this most likely to have happened?" and habits of fresh and accurate thought thus quickly enlivened the formalities of the Greek pictorial theology; formalities themselves beneficent, because restraining by their severity and mystery the wantonness of the newer life. Foolish modern critics have seen nothing in the Byzantine school but a barbarism to be conquered and forgotten. But that school brought to the art-scholars of the thirteenth century, laws which had been serviceable to Phidias, and symbols which had been beautiful to Homer: and methods and habits of pictorial scholarship which gave a refinement of manner to the work of the simplest craftsman, and became an education to the higher artists which no discipline of literature can now bestow, developed themselves in the effort to decipher, and the impulse to re-interpret, the Eleusinian divinity of Byzantine tradition.

88. The words I have just used, "pictorial scholarship," and "pictorial theology," remind me how strange it must appear to you that in this sketch of the intellectual state of Italy in the thirteenth century I have taken no note of literature itself, nor of the fine art of Music with which it was associated in minstrelsy. The corruption of the meaning of the word "clerk," from "a chosen person" to "a learned one," partly indicates the position of literature in the war between the golden crest and scarlet cap; but in the higher ranks, literature and music became the grace of the noble's life, or the occupation of the monk's, without forming any separate class, or exercising any materially visible political power. Masons or butchers might establish a government,—but never troubadours: and though a good knight held his education to be imperfect unless he could write a sonnet and sing it, he did not esteem his castle to be at the mercy of the "editor" of a manuscript. He might indeed owe his life to the fidelity of a minstrel, or be guided in his policy by the wit of a clown; but he was not the slave of sensual music, or vulgar literature, and never allowed his Saturday reviewer to appear at table without the cock's comb.

89. On the other hand, what was noblest in thought or saying was in those times as little attended to as it is now. I do not feel sure that, even in after times, the poem of Dante has had any political effect on Italy; but at all events, in his life, even at Verona, where he was treated most kindly, he had not half so much influence with Can Grande as the rough Count of Castelbarco, not one of whose words was ever written, or now remains; and whose portrait, by no means that of a man of literary genius, almost disfigures, by its plainness, the otherwise grave and perfect beauty of his tomb.

LECTURE IV.
PARTED PER PALE.

90. The chart of Italian intellect and policy which I have endeavoured to put into form in the last three lectures, may, I hope, have given you a clear idea of the subordinate, yet partly antagonistic, position which the artist, or merchant,—whom in my present lecture I shall class together,—occupied, with respect to the noble and priest. As an honest labourer, he was opposed to the violence of pillage, and to the folly of pride: as an honest thinker, he was likely to discover any latent absurdity in the stories he had to represent in their nearest likelihood; and to be himself moved strongly by the true meaning of events which he was striving to make ocularly manifest. The painter terrified himself with his own fiends, and reproved or comforted himself by the lips of his own saints, far more profoundly than any verbal preacher; and thus, whether as craftsman or inventor, was likely to be foremost in defending the laws of his city, or directing its reformation.

91. The contest of the craftsman with the pillaging soldier is typically represented by the war of the Lombard League with Frederick II.; and that of the craftsman with the hypocritical priest, by the war of the Pisans with Gregory IX. (1241). But in the present lecture I wish only to fix your attention on the revolutions in Florence, which indicated, thus early, the already established ascendancy of the moral forces which were to put an end to open robber-soldiership; and at least to compel the assertion of some higher principle in war, if not, as in some distant day may be possible, the cessation of war itself.

The most important of these revolutions was virtually that of which I before spoke to you, taking place in mid-thirteenth century, in the year 1250,—a very memorable one for Christendom, and the very crisis of vital change in its methods of economy, and conceptions of art.

92. Observe, first, the exact relations at that time of Christian and Profane Chivalry. St. Louis, in the winter of 1248-9, lay in the isle of Cyprus, with his crusading army. He had trusted to Providence for provisions; and his army was starving. The profane German emperor, Frederick II., was at war with Venice, but gave a safe-conduct to the Venetian ships, which enabled them to carry food to Cyprus, and to save St. Louis and his crusaders. Frederick had been for half his life excommunicate,—and the Pope (Innocent IV.) at deadly spiritual and temporal war with him;—spiritually, because he had brought Saracens into Apulia; temporally, because the Pope wanted Apulia for himself. St. Louis and his mother both wrote to Innocent, praying him to be reconciled to the kind heretic who had saved the whole crusading army. But the Pope remained implacably thundrous; and Frederick, weary of

quarrel, stayed quiet in one of his Apulian castles for a year. The repose of infidelity is seldom cheerful, unless it be criminal. Frederick had much to repent of, much to regret, nothing to hope, and nothing to do. At the end of his year's quiet he was attacked by dysentery, and so made his final peace with the Pope, and heaven,—aged fifty-six.

93. Meantime St. Louis had gone on into Egypt, had got his army defeated, his brother killed, and himself carried captive. You may be interested in seeing, in the leaf of his psalter which I have laid on the table, the death of that brother set down in golden letters, between the common letters of ultramarine, on the eighth of February.

94. Providence, defied by Frederick, and trusted in by St. Louis, made such arrangements for them both; Providence not in anywise regarding the opinions of either king, but very much regarding the facts, that the one had no business in Egypt, nor the other in Apulia.

No two kings, in the history of the world, could have been happier, or more useful, than these two might have been, if they only had had the sense to stay in their own capitals, and attend to their own affairs. But they seem only to have been born to show what grievous results, under the power of discontented imagination, a Christian could achieve by faith, and a philosopher by reason. {1}

{Footnote 1: It must not be thought that this is said in disregard of the nobleness of either of these two glorious Kings. Among the many designs of past years, one of my favorites was to write a life of Frederick II. But I hope that both his, and that of Henry II. of England, will soon be written now, by a man who loves them as well as I do, and knows them far better.}

95. The death of Frederick II. virtually ended the soldier power in Florence; and the mercantile power assumed the authority it thenceforward held, until, in the hands of the Medici, it destroyed the city.

We will now trace the course and effects of the three revolutions which closed the reign of War, and crowned the power of Peace.

96. In the year 1248, while St. Louis was in Cyprus, I told you Frederick was at war with Venice. He was so because she stood, if not as the leader, at least as the most important ally, of the great Lombard mercantile league against the German military power.

That league consisted essentially of Venice, Milan, Bologna, and Genoa, in alliance with the Pope; the Imperial or Ghibelline towns were, Padua and Verona under Ezzelin; Mantua, Pisa, and Siena. I do not name the minor towns of north Italy which associated themselves with each party: get only the main localities of the contest well into your minds. It was all concentrated in the furious hostility of Genoa and Pisa; Genoa fighting really very piously for the Pope, as well as for herself; Pisa for her own hand, and for the Emperor as much as suited her. The mad little sea falcon never caught sight of another water-bird on the wing, but she must hawk at it; and as an ally of the Emperor, balanced Venice and Genoa with her single strength. And so it came to pass that the victory of either the Guelph or Ghibelline party depended on the final action of Florence.

97. Florence meanwhile was fighting with herself, for her own amusement. She was nominally at the head of the Guelphic League in Tuscany; but this only meant that she hated Siena and Pisa, her southern and western neighbours. She had never declared openly against the Emperor. On the contrary, she always recognized his authority, in an imaginative manner, as representing that of the Caesars. She spent her own energy chiefly in street-fighting,—the death of Buondelmonti in 1215 having been the root of a series of quarrels among her nobles which gradually took the form of contests of honour; and were a kind of accidental tournaments, fought to the death, because they could not be exciting or dignified enough on any other condition. And thus the manner of life came to be customary, which you have accurately, with its consequences, pictured by Shakspeare. Samson bites his thumb at Abraham, and presently the streets are impassable in battle. The quarrel in the Canongate between the Leslies and Seytons, in Scott's 'Abbot,' represents the same temper; and marks also, what Shakspeare did not so distinctly, because it would have interfered with the domestic character of his play, the connection of these private quarrels with political divisions which paralyzed the entire body of the State.—Yet these political schisms, in the earlier days of Italy, never reached the bitterness of Scottish feud, {1} because they were never so sincere. Protestant and Catholic Scotsmen faithfully believed each other to be servants of the devil; but the Guelph and Ghibelline of Florence each respected, in the other, the fidelity to the Emperor, or piety towards the Pope, which he found it convenient, for the time, to dispense with in his own person. The street fighting was therefore more general, more chivalric, more good-humoured; a word of offence set all the noblesse of the town on fire; every one rallied to his post; fighting began at once in half a dozen places of recognized convenience, but ended in the evening; and, on the following day, the leaders determined in contended truce who had fought best, buried their dead triumphantly, and better fortified any weak points, which the events of the previous day had exposed at their palace corners. Florentine dispute was apt to centre itself about the gate of St. Peter, {2} the tower of the cathedral, or the fortress-palace of the Uberti, (the family of Dante's Bellincion Berti and of Farinata), which occupied the site of the present Palazzo Vecchio. But the streets of Siena seem to have afforded better barricade practice. They are as steep as they are narrow—extremely both; and the projecting stones on their palace

fronts, which were left, in building, to sustain, on occasion, the barricade beams across the streets, are to this day important features in their architecture.

{Footnote 1: Distinguish always the personal from the religious feud; personal feud is more treacherous and violent in Italy than in Scotland; but not the political or religious feud, unless involved with vast material interests.}

{Footnote 2: Sismondi, vol. ii., chap. ii.; G. Villani, vi., 33.}

98. Such being the general state of matters in Florence, in this year 1248, Frederick writes to the Uberti, who headed the Ghibellines, to engage them in serious effort to bring the city distinctly to the Imperial side. He was besieging Parma; and sent his natural son, Frederick, king of Antioch, with sixteen hundred German knights, to give the Ghibellines assured preponderance in the next quarrel.

The Uberti took arms before their arrival; rallied all their Ghibelline friends into a united body, and so attacked and carried the Guelph barricades, one by one, till their antagonists, driven together by local defeat, stood in consistency as complete as their own, by the gate of St. Peter, 'Scheraggio.' Young Frederick, with his German riders, arrived at this crisis; the Ghibellines opening the gates to him; the Guelphs, nevertheless, fought at their outmost barricade for four days more; but at last, tired, withdrew from the city, in a body, on the night of Candlemas, 2nd February, 1248; leaving the Ghibellines and their German friends to work their pleasure,—who immediately set themselves to throw down the Guelph palaces, and destroyed six-and-thirty of them, towers and all, with the good help of Niccola Pisano,—for this is the occasion of that beautiful piece of new engineering of his.

99. It is the first interference of the Germans in Florentine affairs which belongs to the real cycle of modern history. Six hundred years later, a troop of German riders entered Florence again, to restore its Grand Duke; and our warmhearted and loving English poetess, looking on from Casa Guidi windows, gives the said Germans many hard words, and thinks her darling Florentines entirely innocent in the matter. But if she had had clear eyes, (yeux de lin {1} the Romance of the Rose calls them,) she would have seen that white-coated cavalry with its heavy guns to be nothing more than the rear-guard of young Frederick of Antioch; and that Florence's own Ghibellines had opened her gates to them. Destiny little regards cost of time; she does her justice at that telescopic distance just as easily and accurately as close at hand.

{Footnote 1: Lynx.}

100. "Frederick of *Antioch*." Note the titular coincidence. The disciples were called Christians first in Antioch; here we have our lieutenant of Antichrist also named from that town. The anti-Christian Germans got into Florence upon Sunday morning; the Guelphs fought on till Wednesday, which was Candlemas;—the Tower of the Death-watch was thrown down next day. It was so called because it stood on the Piazza of St John; and all dying people in Florence called on St. John for help; and looked, if it might be, to the top of this highest and best-built of towers. The wicked anti-Christian Ghibellines, Nicholas of Pisa helping, cut the side of it "so that the tower might fall on the Baptistery. But as it pleased God, for better reverencing of the blessed St. John, the tower, which was a hundred and eighty feet high, as it was coming down, plainly appeared to eschew the holy church, and turned aside, and fell right across the square; at which all the Florentines marvelled, (pious or impious,) and the *people* (anti-Ghibelline) were greatly delighted."

101. I have no doubt that this story is apocryphal, not only in its attribution of these religious scruples to the falling tower; but in its accusation of the Ghibellines as having definitely intended the destruction of the Baptistery. It is only modern reformers who feel the absolute need of enforcing their religious opinions in so practical a manner. Such a piece of sacrilege would have been revolting to Farinata; how much more to the group of Florentines whose temper is centrally represented by Dante's, to all of whom their "bel San Giovanni" was dear, at least for its beauty, if not for its sanctity. And Niccola himself was too good a workman to become the instrument of the destruction of so noble a work,—not to insist on the extreme probability that he was also too good an engineer to have had his purpose, if once fixed, thwarted by any tenderness in the conscience of the collapsing tower. The tradition itself probably arose after the rage of the exiled Ghibellines had half consented to the destruction, on political grounds, of Florence itself; but the form it took is of extreme historical value, indicating thus early at least the suspected existence of passions like those of the Cromwellian or Garibaldian soldiery in the Florentine noble; and the distinct character of the Ghibelline party as not only anti-Papal, but profane.

102. Upon the castles, and the persons of their antagonists, however, the pride, or fear, of the Ghibellines had little mercy; and in their day of triumph they provoked against themselves nearly every rational as well as religious person in the commonwealth. They despised too much the force of the newly-risen popular power, founded on economy, sobriety, and common sense; and, alike by impertinence and pillage, increased the irritation of the civil body; until, as aforesaid, on the 20th October, 1250, all the rich burgesses of Florence took arms; met in the square before the church of Santa Croce, ("where," says Sismondi, "the republic of the dead is still assembled today,") thence traversed the city to the palace of the Ghibelline

podesta; forced him to resign; named Uberto of Lucca in his place, under the title of Captain of the People; divided themselves into twenty companies, each, in its own district of the city, having its captain {1} and standard; and elected a council of twelve ancients, constituting a seniory or signoria, to deliberate on and direct public affairs.

{Footnote 1: 'Corporal,' literally'.}

103. What a perfectly beautiful republican movement! thinks Sismondi, seeing, in all this, nothing but the energy of a multitude; and entirely ignoring the peculiar capacity of this Florentine mob,—capacity of two virtues, much forgotten by modern republicanism,—order, namely; and obedience; together with the peculiar instinct of this Florentine multitude, which not only felt itself to need captains, but knew where to find them.

104. Hubert of Lucca—How came they, think you, to choose *him* out of a stranger city, and that a poorer one than their own? Was there no Florentine then, of all this rich and eager crowd, who was fit to govern Florence?

I cannot find any account of this Hubert, Bright mind, of Ducca; Villani says simply of him, "Fu il primo capitano di Firenze."

They hung a bell for him in the Campanile of the Lion, and gave him the flag of Florence to bear; and before the day was over, that 20th of October, he had given every one of the twenty companies their flags also. And the bearings of the said gonfalons were these. I will give you this heraldry as far as I can make it out from Villani; it will be very useful to us afterwards; I leave the Italian when I cannot translate it:—

105. A. Sesto, (sixth part of the city,) of the other side of Arno.

Gonfalon 1. Gules; a ladder, argent.

2. Argent; a scourge, sable.

3. Azure; (una piazza bianca con

nicchi vermigli).

4. Gules; a dragon, vert.

B. Sesto of St. Peter Scheraggio.

1. Azure; a chariot, or.

2. Or; a bull, sable.

3. Argent; a lion rampant, sable.

4. (A lively piece, "pezza gagliarda")

Barry of (how many?) pieces,

argent and sable.

You may as well note at once of this kind of bearing, called 'gagliarda' by Villani, that these groups of piles, pales, bends, and bars, were called in English heraldry 'Restrial bearings,' "in respect of their strength and solid substance, which is able to abide the stresse and force of any triall they shall be put unto." {1} And also that, the number of bars being uncertain, I assume the bearing to be 'barry,' that is, having an even number of bars; had it been odd, as of seven bars, it should have been blazoned, argent; three bars, sable; or, if so divided, sable, three bars argent.

{Footnote 1: Guillim, sect. ii., chap. 3.}

This lively bearing was St. Pulinari's.

C. Sesto of Borgo.

> *1. Or; a viper, vert.*
>
> *2. Argent; a needle, (?) (aguglia)*
>
> *sable.*
>
> *3. Vert; a horse unbridled;*
>
> *draped, argent, a cross,*
>
> *gules.*

D. Sesto of St. Brancazio.

> *1. Vert; a lion rampant, proper.*
>
> *2. Argent; a lion rampant, gules.*
>
> *3. Azure; a lion rampant, argent.*

E. Sesto of the Cathedral gates.

> *1. Azure; a lion (passant?) or.*
>
> *2. Or; a dragon, vert.*
>
> *3. Argent; a lion rampant,*
>
> *azure, crowned, or.*

F. Sesto of St. Peter's gates.

> *1. Or; two keys, gules.*
>
> *2. An Italian (or more definitely*
>
> *a Greek and Etruscan bearing;*
>
> *I do not know how to*

blazon it;) concentric bands,
argent and sable. This is
one of the remains of the
Greek expressions of storm;
hail, or the Trinacrian limbs,
being put on the giant's
shields also. It is connected
besides with the Cretan
labyrinth, and the circles of
the Inferno.
3. Parted per fesse, gules and
vai (I don't know if vai
means grey—not a proper
heraldic colour—or vaire).

106. Of course Hubert of Lucca did not determine these bearings, but took them as he found them, and appointed them for standards; {1} he did the same for all the country parishes, and ordered them to come into the city at need. "And in this manner the old people of Florence ordered itself; and for more strength of the people, they ordered and began to build the palace which is behind the Badia,—that is to say, the one which is of dressed stone, with the tower; for before there was no palace of the commune in Florence, but the signory abode sometimes in one part of the town, sometimes in another.

{Footnote 1: We will examine afterwards the heraldry of the trades, chap, xi., Villani.}

107. "And as the people had now taken state and signory on themselves, they ordered, for greater strength of the people, that all the towers of Florence— and there were many 180 feet high {1}—should be cut down to 75 feet, and no more; and so it was done, and with the stones of them they walled the city on the other side Arno."

{Footnote: 120 braccia.}

108. That last sentence is a significant one. Here is the central expression of the true burgess or townsman temper,—resolute maintenance of fortified

peace. These are the walls which modern republicanism throws down, to make boulevards over their ruins.

109. Such new order being taken, Florence remained quiet for full two months. On the 13th of December, in the same year, died the Emperor Frederick II.; news of his death did not reach Florence till the 7th January, 1251. It had chanced, according to Villani, that on the actual day of his death, his Florentine vice-regent, Rinieri of Montemerlo, was killed by a piece of the vaulting {1} of his room falling on him as he slept. And when the people heard of the Emperor's death, "which was most useful and needful for Holy Church, and for our commune," they took the fall of the roof on his lieutenant as an omen of the extinction of Imperial authority, and resolved to bring home all their Guelphic exiles, and that the Ghibellines should be forced to make peace with them. Which was done, and the peace really lasted for full six months; when, a quarrel chancing with Ghibelline Pistoja, the Florentines, under a Milanese podesta, fought their first properly communal and commercial battle, with great slaughter of Pistojese. Naturally enough, but very unwisely, the Florentine Ghibellines declined to take part in this battle; whereupon the people, returning flushed with victory, drove them all out, and established pure Guelph government in Florence, changing at the same time the flag of the city from gules, a lily argent, to argent, a lily gules; but the most ancient bearing of all, simply parted per pale, argent and gules, remained always on their carroccio of battle,—"Non si muto mai."

{Footnote 1: "Una volta ch' era sopra la camera."}

110. "Non si muto mai." Villani did not know how true his words were. That old shield of Florence, parted per pale, argent and gules, (or our own Saxon Oswald's, parted per pale, or and purpure,) are heraldry changeless in sign; declaring the necessary balance, in ruling men, of the Rational and Imaginative powers; pure Alp, and glowing cloud.

Church and State—Pope and Emperor—Clergy and Laity,—all these are partial, accidental—too often, criminal—oppositions; but the bodily and spiritual elements, seemingly adverse, remain in everlasting harmony,

Not less the new bearing of the shield, the red fleur-de-lys, has another meaning. It is red, not as ecclesiastical, but as free. Not of Guelph against Ghibelline, but of Labourer against Knight. No more his serf, but his minister. His duty no more 'servitium,' but 'ministerium,' 'mestier.' We learn the power of word after word, as of sign after sign, as we follow the traces of this nascent art. I have sketched for you this lily from the base of the tower of Giotto. You may judge by the subjects of the sculpture beside it that it was built just in this fit of commercial triumph; for all the outer bas-reliefs are of trades.

111. Draw that red lily then, and fix it in your minds as the sign of the great change in the temper of Florence, and in her laws, in mid-thirteenth century; and remember also, when you go to Florence and see that mighty tower of the Palazzo Vecchio (noble still, in spite of the calamitous and accursed restorations which have smoothed its rugged outline, and effaced with modern vulgarisms its lovely sculpture)—terminating the shadowy perspectives of the Uffizii, or dominant over the city seen from Fésole or Bellosguardo,—that, as the tower of Giotto is the notablest monument in the world of the Religion of Europe, so, on this tower of the Palazzo Vecchio, first shook itself to the winds the Lily standard of her liberal,— because honest,—commerce.

LECTURE V.
PAX VOBISCUM.

112. My last lecture ended with a sentence which I thought, myself, rather pretty, and quite fit for a popular newspaper, about the 'lily standard of liberal commerce.' But it might occur, and I hope did occur, to some of you, that it would have been more appropriate if the lily had changed colour the other way, from red to white, (instead of white to red,) as a sign of a pacific constitution and kindly national purpose.

113. I believe otherwise, however; and although the change itself was for the sake of change merely, you may see in it, I think, one of the historical coincidences which contain true instruction for us.

Quite one of the chiefest art-mistakes and stupidities of men has been their tendency to dress soldiers in red clothes, and monks, or pacific persons, in black, white, or grey ones. At least half of that mental bias of young people, which sustains the wickedness of war among us at this day, is owing to the prettiness of uniforms. Make all Hussars black, all Guards black, all troops of the line black; dress officers and men, alike, as you would public executioners; and the number of candidates for commissions will be greatly diminished. Habitually, on the contrary, you dress these destructive rustics and their officers in scarlet and gold, but give your productive rustics no costume of honour or beauty; you give your peaceful student a costume which he tucks up to his waist, because he is ashamed of it; and dress your pious rectors, and your sisters of charity, in black, as if it were *their* trade instead of the soldier's to send people to hell, and their own destiny to arrive there.

114. But the investiture of the lily of Florence with scarlet is a symbol,— unintentional, observe, but not the less notable,—of the recovery of human sense and intelligence in this matter. The reign of war was past; this was the sign of it;—the red glow, not now of the Towers of Dis, but of the Carita, "che appena fora dentro al fuoco nota." And a day is coming, be assured, when the kings of Europe will dress their peaceful troops beautifully; will clothe their peasant girls "in scarlet, with other delights," and "put on ornaments of gold upon *their* apparel;" when the crocus and the lily will not be the only living things dressed daintily in our land, and the glory of the wisest monarchs be indeed, in that their people, like themselves, shall be, at least in some dim likeness, "arrayed like one of these."

115. But as for the immediate behaviour of Florence herself, with her new standard, its colour was quite sufficiently significant in that old symbolism, when the first restrial bearing was drawn by dying fingers dipped in blood. The Guelphic revolution had put her into definite political opposition with

her nearest, and therefore,—according to the custom and Christianity of the time,—her hatefullest, neighbours,—Pistoja, Pisa, Siena, and Volterra. What glory might not be acquired, what kind purposes answered, by making pacific mercantile states also of those benighted towns! Besides, the death of the Emperor had thrown his party everywhere into discouragement; and what was the use of a flag which flew no farther than over the new palazzo?

116. Accordingly, in the next year, the pacific Florentines began by ravaging the territory of Pistoja; then attacked the Pisans at Pontadera, and took 3000 prisoners; and finished by traversing, and eating up all that could be ate in, the country of Siena; besides beating the Sienese under the castle of Montalcino. Returning in triumph after these benevolent operations, they resolved to strike a new piece of money in memory of them,—the golden Florin!

117. This coin I have placed in your room of study, to be the first of the series of coins which I hope to arrange for you, not chronologically, but for the various interest, whether as regards art or history, which they should possess in your general studies. "The Florin of Florence," (says Sismondi), "through all the monetary revolutions of all neighbouring countries, and while the bad faith of governments adulterated their coin from one end of Europe to the other, has always remained the same; it is, to-day," (I don't know when, exactly, he wrote this,—but it doesn't matter), "of the same weight, and bears the same name and the same stamp, which it did when it was struck in 1252." It was gold of the purest title (24 carats), weighed the eighth of an ounce, and carried, as you see, on one side the image of St. John Baptist, on the other the Fleur-de-lys. It is the coin which Chaucer takes for the best representation of beautiful money in the Pardoner's Tale: this, in his judgment, is the fairest mask of Death. Villani's relation of its moral and commercial effect at Tunis is worth translating, being in the substance of it, I doubt not, true.

118. "And these new florins beginning to scatter through the world, some of them got to Tunis, in Barbary; and the King of Tunis, who was a worthy and wise lord, was greatly pleased with them, and had them tested; and finding them of fine gold, he praised them much, and had the legend on them interpreted to him,—to wit, on one side 'St. John Baptist,' on the other 'Florentia.' So seeing they were pieces of Christian money, he sent for the Pisan merchants, who were free of his port, and much before the King (and also the Florentines traded in Tunis through Pisan agents),—{see these hot little Pisans, how they are first everywhere,}—and asked of them what city it was among the Christians which made the said florins. And the Pisans answered in spite and envy, 'They are our land Arabs.' The King answered wisely, "It does not appear to me Arab's money; you Pisans, what golden money have *you* got?" Then they were confused, and knew not what to

answer. So he asked if there was any Florentine among them. And there was found a merchant from the other-side-Arno, by name Peter Balducci, discreet and wise. The King asked him of the state and being of Florence, of which the Pisans made their Arabs,—who answered him wisely, showing the power and magnificence of Florence; and how Pisa, in comparison, was not, either in land or people, the half of Florence; and that they had no golden money; and that the gold of which those florins had been made was gained by the Florentines above and beyond them, by many victories. Wherefore the said Pisans were put to shame, and the King, both by reason of the florin, and for the words of our wise citizen, made the Florentines free, and appointed for them their own Fondaco, and church, in Tunis, and gave them privileges like the Pisans. And this we know for a truth from the same Peter, having been in company with him at the office of the Priors."

119. I cannot tell you what the value of the piece was at this time: the sentence with which Sismondi concludes his account of it being only useful as an example of the total ignorance of the laws of currency in which many even of the best educated persons at the present day remain.

"Its value," he says always the same, "answers to eleven francs forty centimes of France."

But all that can be scientifically said of any piece of money is that it contains a given weight of a given metal. Its value in other coins, other metals, or other general produce, varies not only from day to day, but from instant to instant.

120. With this coin of Florence ought in justice to be ranked the Venetian zecchin; {1} but of it I can only thus give you account in another place,—for I must at once go on now to tell you the first use I find recorded, as being made by the Florentines of their new money.

{Footnote 1: In connection with the Pisans' insulting intention by their term of Arabs, remember that the Venetian 'zecca,' (mint) came from the Arabic 'sehk,' the steel die used in coinage.}

They pursued in the years 1253 and 1254 their energetic promulgation of peace. They ravaged the lands of Pistoja so often, that the Pistojese submitted themselves, on condition of receiving back their Guelph exiles, and admitting a Florentine garrison into Pistoja. Next they attacked Monte Reggione, the March-fortress of the Sienese; and pressed it so vigorously that Siena was fain to make peace too, on condition of ceasing her alliance with the Ghibellines. Next they ravaged the territory of Volterra: the townspeople, confident in the strength of their rock fortress, came out to give battle; the Florentines beat them up the hill, and entered the town gates with the fugitives.

121. And, for note to this sentence, in my long-since-read volume of Sismondi, I find a cross-fleury at the bottom of the page, with the date 1254 underneath it; meaning that I was to remember that year as the beginning of Christian warfare. For little as you may think it, and grotesquely opposed as this ravaging of their neighbours' territories may seem to their pacific mission, this Florentine army is fighting in absolute good faith. Partly self-deceived, indeed, by their own ambition, and by their fiery natures, rejoicing in the excitement of battle, they have nevertheless, in this their "year of victories,"—so they ever afterwards called it,—no occult or malignant purpose. At least, whatever is occult or malignant is also unconscious; not now in cruel, but in kindly jealousy of their neighbours, and in a true desire to communicate and extend to them the privileges of their own new artizan government, the Trades of Florence have taken arms. They are justly proud of themselves; rightly assured of the wisdom of the change they have made; true to each other for the time, and confident in the future. No army ever fought in better cause, or with more united heart. And accordingly they meet with no check, and commit no error; from tower to tower of the field fortresses,—from gate to gate of the great cities,—they march in one continuous and daily more splendid triumph, yet in gentle and perfect discipline; and now, when they have entered Volterra with her fugitives, after stress of battle, not a drop of blood is shed, nor a single house pillaged, nor is any other condition of peace required than the exile of the Ghibelline nobles. You may remember, as a symbol of the influence of Christianity in this result, that the Bishop of Volterra, with his clergy, came out in procession to meet them as they began to run {1} the streets, and obtained this mercy; else the old habits of pillage would have prevailed.

{Footnote 1: Corsona la citta senza contesto niuno."—*Villani*.}

122. And from Volterra, the Florentine army entered on the territory of Pisa; and now with so high prestige, that the Pisans at once sent ambassadors to them with keys in their hands, in token of submission. And the Florentines made peace with them, on condition that the Pisans should let the Florentine merchandize pass in and out without tax;—should use the same weights as Florence,—the same cloth measure,—and the same alloy of money.

123. You see that Mr. Adam Smith was not altogether the originator of the idea of free trade; and six hundred years have passed without bringing Europe generally to the degree of mercantile intelligence, as to weights and currency, which Florence had in her year of victories.

The Pisans broke this peace two years afterwards, to help the Emperor Manfred; whereupon the Florentines attacked them instantly again; defeated them on the Serchio, near Lucca; entered the Pisan territory by the Val di Serchio; and there, cutting down a great pine tree, struck their florins on the stump of it, putting, for memory, under the feet of the St. John, a trefoil "in guise of a little tree." And note here the difference between artistic and mechanical coinage. The Florentines, using pure gold, and thin, can strike their coin anywhere, with only a wooden anvil, and their engraver is ready on the instant to make such change in the stamp as may record any new triumph. Consider the vigour, popularity, pleasantness of an art of coinage thus ductile to events, and easy in manipulution.

124. It is to be observed also that a thin gold coinage like that of the English angel, and these Italian zecchins, is both more convenient and prettier than the massive gold of the Greeks, often so small that it drops through the fingers, and, if of any size, inconveniently large in value.

125. It was in the following year, 1255, that the Florentines made the noblest use of their newly struck florins, so far as I know, ever recorded in any history; and a Florentine citizen made as noble refusal of them. You will find the two stories in Giovanni Villani, Book 6th, chapters 61, 62. One or two important facts are added by Sismondi, but without references. I take his statement as on the whole trustworthy, using Villani's authority wherever it reaches; one or two points I have farther to explain to you myself as I go on.

126. The first tale shows very curiously the mercenary and independent character of warfare, as it now was carried on by the great chiefs, whether Guelph or Ghibelline. The Florentines wanted to send a troop of five hundred horse to assist Orvieto, a Guelph town, isolated on its rock, and at present harrassed upon it. They gave command of this troop to the Knight Guido Guerra de' Conti Guidi, and he and his riders set out for Orvieto by the Umbrian road, through Arezzo, which was at peace with Florence, though a Ghibelline town. The Guelph party within the town asked help from the passing Florentine battalion; and Guido Guerra, without any authority for such action, used the troop of which he was in command in their favour, and drove out the Ghibellines. Sismondi does not notice what is quite one of the main points in the matter, that this troop of horse must have been mainly composed of Count Guido's own retainers, and not of Florentine citizens, who would not have cared to leave their business on such a far-off quest as this help to Orvieto. However, Arezzo is thus brought over to the Florentine interest; and any other Italian state would have been sure, while it disclaimed the Count's independent action, to keep the advantage of it. Not so Florence. She is entirely resolved, in these years of victory, to do justice to all men so far she understands it; and in this case it will give her some trouble to do it, and worse,—cost her some of her fine new florins. For her counter-mandate is quite powerless with Guido Guerra. He has taken Arezzo mainly with his own men, and means to stay there, thinking that the Florentines, if even they do not abet him, will take no practical steps against him. But he does not know this newly risen clan of military merchants, who

quite clearly understand what honesty means, and will put themselves out of their way to keep their faith. Florence calls out her trades instantly, and with gules, a dragon vert, and or, a bull sable, they march, themselves, angrily up the Val d'Arno, replace the adverse Ghibellines in Arezzo, and send Master Guido de' Conti Guido about his business. But the prettiest and most curious part of the whole story is their equity even to him, after he had given them all this trouble. They entirely recognize the need he is under of getting meat, somehow, for the mouths of these five hundred riders of his; also they hold him still their friend, though an unmanageable one; and admit with praise what of more or less patriotic and Guelphic principle may be at the root of his disobedience. So when he claims twelve thousand lire,—roughly, some two thousand pounds of money at present value,—from the Guelphs of Arezzo for his service, and the Guelphs, having got no good of it, owing to this Florentine interference, object to paying him, the Florentines themselves lend them the money,—and are never paid a farthing of it back.

127. There is a beautiful "investment of capital" for your modern merchant to study! No interest thought of, and little hope of ever getting back the principal. And yet you will find that there were no mercantile "panics," in Florence in those days, nor failing bankers, {1} nor "clearings out of this establishment—any reasonable offer accepted."

{Footnote: Some account of the state of modern British business in this kind will be given, I hope, in some number of "Fors Clavigera" for this year, 1874.}

128. But the second story, of a private Florentine citizen, is better still.

In that campaign against Pisa in which the florins were struck on the root of pine, the conditions of peace had been ratified by the surrender to Florence of the Pisan fortress of Mutrona, which commanded a tract of seaboard below Pisa, of great importance for the Tuscan trade. The Florentines had stipulated for the right not only of holding, but of destroying it, if they chose; and in their Council of Ancients, after long debate, it was determined to raze it, the cost of its garrison being troublesome, and the freedom of seaboard all that the city wanted. But the Pisans feeling the power that the fortress had against them in case of future war, and doubtful of the issue of council at Florence, sent a private negotiator to the member of the Council of Ancients who was known to have most influence, though one of the poorest of them, Aldobrandino Ottobuoni; and offered him four thousand golden florins if he would get the vote passed to raze Mutrona. The vote *had* passed the evening before. Aldobrandino dismissed the Pisan ambassador in silence, returned instantly into the council, and without saying anything of the offer that had been made to him, got them to reconsider their vote, and showed them such reason for keeping Mutrona in its strength, that the vote for its destruction was rescinded. "And note thou, oh reader," says Villani, "the virtue of such a citizen, who, not being rich in substance, had yet such continence and loyalty for his state."

129. You might, perhaps, once, have thought me detaining you needlessly with these historical details, little bearing, it is commonly supposed, on the subject of art. But you are, I trust, now in some degree persuaded that no art, Florentine or any other, can be understood without knowing these sculptures and mouldings of the national soul. You remember I first begun this large digression when it became a question with us why some of Giovanni Pisano's sepulchral work had been destroyed at Perugia. And now we shall get our first gleam of light on the matter, finding similar operations carried on in Florence. For a little while after this speech in the Council of Ancients, Aldobrandino died, and the people, at public cost, built him a tomb of marble, "higher than any other" in the church of Santa Reparata, engraving on it these verses, which I leave you to construe, for I cannot:—

Fons est supremus Aldobrandino amoenus.

Ottoboni natus, a bono civita datus.

Only I suppose the pretty word 'amoenus' may be taken as marking the delightfulness and sweetness of character which had won all men's love, more, even, than their gratitude.

130. It failed of its effect, however, on the Tuscan aristocratic mind. For, when, after the battle of the Arbia, the Ghibellines had again their own way in Florence, though Ottobuoni had been then dead three years, they beat down his tomb, pulled the dead body out of it, dragged it—by such tenure as it might still possess—through the city, and threw the fragments of it into ditches. It is a memorable parallel to the treatment of the body of Cromwell by our own Cavaliers; and indeed it seems to me one of the highest forms of laudatory epitaph upon a man, that his body should be thus torn from its rest. For he can hardly have spent his life better than in drawing on himself the kind of enmity which can so be gratified; and for the most loving of lawgivers, as of princes, the most enviable and honourable epitaph has always been

{Greek: "oide plitai anton emisoun anton."

131. Not but that pacific Florence, in her pride of victory, was beginning to show unamiableness of temper also, on her so equitable side. It is perhaps worth noticing, for the sake of the name of Correggio, that in 1257, when Matthew Correggio, of Parma, was the Podesta of Florence, the Florentines determined to destroy the castle and walls of Poggibonzi, suspected of Ghibelline tendency, though the Poggibonzi people came with "coregge in collo," leathern straps round their necks, to ask that their cattle might be

spared. And the heartburnings between the two parties went on, smouldering hotter and hotter, till July, 1258, when the people having discovered secret dealings between the Uberti and the Emperor Manfred, and the Uberti refusing to obey citation to the popular tribunals, the trades ran to arms, attacked the Uberti palace, killed a number of their people, took prisoner, Uberto of the Uberti, Hubert of the Huberts, or Bright-mind of the Bright-minds, with 'Mangia degl' Infangati, ('Gobbler {1} of the dirty ones' this knight's name sounds like,)—and after they had confessed their guilt, beheaded them in St. Michael's corn-market; and all the rest of the Uberti and Ghibelline families were driven out of Florence, and their palaces pulled down, and the walls towards Siena built with the stones of them; and two months afterwards, the people suspecting the Abbot of Vallombrosa of treating with the Ghibellines, took him, and tortured him; and he confessing under torture, "at the cry of the people, they beheaded him in the square of St. Apollinare." For which unexpected piece of clangorous impiety the Florentines were excommunicated, besides drawing upon themselves the steady enmity of Pavia, the Abbot's native town; "and indeed people say the Abbot was innocent, though he belonged to a great Ghibelline house. And for this sin, and for many others done by the wicked people, many wise persons say that God, for Divine judgment, permitted upon the said people the revenge and slaughter of Monteaperti."

{Footnote: At least, the compound 'Mangia-pane,' 'munch-bread,' stands still for a good-for-nothing fellow.}

132. The sentence which I have last read introduces, as you must at once have felt, a new condition of things. Generally, I have spoken of the Ghibellines as infidel, or impious; and for the most part they represent, indeed, the resistance of kingly to priestly power. But, in this action of Florence, we have the rise of another force against the Church, in the end to be much more fatal to it, that of popular intelligence and popular passion. I must for the present, however, return to our immediate business; and ask you to take note of the effect, on actually existing Florentine architecture, of the political movements of the ten years we have been studying.

133. In the revolution of Candlemas, 1248, the successful Ghibellines throw down thirty-six of the Guelph palaces.

And in the revolution of July, 1258, the successful Guelphs throw down *all* the Ghibelline palaces.

Meantime the trades, as against the Knights Castellans, have thrown down the tops of all the towers above seventy-five feet high.

And we shall presently have a proposal, after the battle of the Arbia, to throw down Florence altogether.

134. You think at first that this is remarkably like the course of republican reformations in the present day? But there is a wide difference. In the first place, the palaces and towers are not thrown down in mere spite or desire of ruin, but after quite definite experience of their danger to the State, and positive dejection of boiling lead and wooden logs from their machicolations upon the heads below. In the second place, nothing is thrown down without complete certainty on the part of the overthrowers that they are able, and willing, to build as good or better things instead; which, if any like conviction exist in the minds of modern republicans, is a wofully ill-founded one: and lastly, these abolitions of private wealth were coincident with a widely spreading disposition to undertake, as I have above noticed, works of public utility, *from which no dividends were to be received by any of the shareholders*; and for the execution of which the *builders received no commission on the cost*, but payment at the rate of so much a day, carefully adjusted to the exertion of real power and intelligence.

135. We must not, therefore, without qualification blame, though we may profoundly regret, the destructive passions of the thirteenth century. The architecture of the palaces thus destroyed in Florence contained examples of the most beautiful round-arched work that had been developed by the Norman schools; and was in some cases adorned with a barbaric splendour, and fitted into a majesty of strength which, so far as I can conjecture the effect of it from the few now existing traces, must have presented some of the most impressive aspects of street edifice ever existent among civil societies.

136. It may be a temporary relief for you from the confusion of following the giddy successions of Florentine temper, if I interrupt, in this place, my history of the city by some inquiry into technical points relating to the architecture of these destroyed palaces. Their style is familiar to us, indeed, in a building of which it is difficult to believe the early date,—the leaning tower of Pisa. The lower stories of it are of the twelfth century, and the open arcades of the cathedrals of Pisa and Lucca, as well as the lighter construction of the spire of St. Niccol, at Pisa, (though this was built in continuation of the older style by Niccola himself,) all represent to you, though in enriched condition, the general manner of buidling in palaces of the Norman period in Val d'Arno. That of the Tosinghi, above the old market in Florence, is especially mentioned by Villani, as more than a hundred feet in height, entirely built with little pillars, (colonnelli,) of marble. On their splendid masonry was founded the exquisiteness of that which immediately succeeded them, of which the date is fixed by definite examples both in Verona and Florence, and which still exists in noble masses in the retired streets and courts of either city; too soon superseded, in the great thoroughfares, by the effeminate and monotonous luxury of Venetian renaissance, or by the heaps

of quarried stone which rise into the ruggedness of their native cliffs, in the Pitti and Strozzi palaces.

LECTURE VI.
MARBLE COUCHANT.

137. I told you in my last lecture that the exquisiteness of Florentine thirteenth century masonry was founded on the strength and splendour of that which preceded it.

I use the word 'founded' in a literal as well as figurative sense. While the merchants, in their year of victories, threw down the walls of the war-towers, they as eagerly and diligently set their best craftsmen to lift higher the walls of their churches. For the most part, the Early Norman or Basilican forms were too low to please them in their present enthusiasm. Their pride, as well as their piety, desired that these stones of their temples might be goodly; and all kinds of junctions, insertions, refittings, and elevations were undertaken; which, the genius of the people being always for mosaic, are so perfectly executed, and mix up twelfth and thirteenth century work in such intricate harlequinade, that it is enough to drive a poor antiquary wild.

138. I have here in my hand, however, a photograph of a small church, which shows you the change at a glance, and attests it in a notable manner.

You know Hubert of Lucca was the first captain of the Florentine people, and the march in which they struck their florin on the pine trunk was through Lucca, on Pisa.

Now here is a little church in Lucca, of which the lower half of the façade is of the twelfth century, and the top, built by the Florentines, in the thirteenth, and sealed for their own by two fleur-de-lys, let into its masonry. The most important difference, marking the date, is in the sculpture of the heads which carry the archivolts. But the most palpable difference is in the Cyclopean simplicity of irregular bedding in the lower story; and the delicate bands of alternate serpentine and marble, which follow the horizontal or couchant placing of the stones above.

139. Those of you who, interested in English Gothic, have visited Tuscany, are, I think, always offended at first, if not in permanence, by these horizontal stripes of her marble walls. Twenty-two years ago I quoted, in vol. i. of the "Stones of Venice," Professor Willis's statement that "a practice more destructive of architectural grandeur could hardly be conceived;" and I defended my favourite buildings against that judgement, first by actual comparison in the plate opposite the page, of a piece of them with an example of our modern grandeur; secondly, (vol. i., chap. v.,) by a comparison of their aspect with that of the building of the grandest piece of wall in the Alps,—that Matterhorn in which you all have now learned to take

some gymnastic interest; and thirdly, (vol. i., chap. xxvi.,) by reference to the use of barred colours, with delight, by Giotto and all subsequent colourists.

140. But it did not then occur to me to ask, much as I always disliked the English Perpendicular, what would have been the effect on the spectator's mind, had the buildings been striped vertically instead of horizontally; nor did I then know, or in the least imagine, how much *practical* need there was for reference from the structure of the edifice to that of the cliff; and how much the permanence, as well as propriety, of structure depended on the stones being *couchant* in the wall, as they had been in the quarry: to which subject I wish to-day to direct your attention.

141. You will find stated with as much clearness as I am able, in the first and fifth lectures in "Aratra Pentelíci," the principles of architectural design to which, in all my future teaching, I shall have constantly to appeal; namely, that architecture consists distinctively in the adaptation of form to resist force;—that, practically, it may be always thought of as doing this by the ingenious adjustment of various pieces of solid material; that the perception of this ingenious adjustment, or structure, is to be always joined with our admiration of the superadded ornament; and that all delightful ornament is the honouring of such useful structures; but that the beauty of the ornament itself is independent of the structure, and arrived at by powers of mind of a very different class from those which are necessary to give skill in architecture proper.

142. During the course of this last summer I have been myself very directly interested in some of the quite elementary processes of true architecture. I have been building a little pier into Coniston Lake, and various walls and terraces in a steeply sloping garden, all which had to be constructed of such rough stones as lay nearest. Under the dextrous hands of a neighbour farmer's son, the pier projected, and the walls rose, as if enchanted; every stone taking its proper place, and the loose dyke holding itself as firmly upright as if the gripping cement of the Florentine towers had fastened it. My own better acquaintance with the laws of gravity and of statics did not enable me, myself, to build six inches of dyke that would stand; and all the decoration possible under the circumstances consisted in turning the lichened sides of the stones outwards. And yet the noblest conditions of building in the world are nothing more than the gradual adornment, by play of the imagination, of materials first arranged by this natural instinct of adjustment. You must not lose sight of the instinct of building, but you must not think the play of the imagination depends upon it. Intelligent laying of stones is always delightful; but the fancy must not be limited to its contemplation.

{Illustration: PLATE V.—DOOR OF THE BAPTISTERY. PISA.}

143. In the more elaborate architecture of my neighbourhood, I have taken pleasure these many years; one of the first papers I ever wrote on architecture was a study of the Westmoreland cottage;—properly, observe, the cottage of West-mereland, of the land of western lakes. Its principal feature is the projecting porch at its door, formed by two rough slabs of Coniston slate, set in a blunt gable; supported, if far projecting, by two larger masses for uprights. A disciple of Mr. Pugin would delightedly observe that the porch of St. Zeno at Verona was nothing more than the decoration of this construction; but you do not suppose that the first idea of putting two stones together to keep off rain was all on which the sculptor of St. Zeno wished to depend for your entertainment.

144. Perhaps you may most clearly understand the real connection between structure and decoration by considering all architecture as a kind of book, which must be properly bound indeed, and in which the illumination of the pages has distinct reference in all its forms to the breadth of the margins and length of the sentences; but is itself free to follow its own quite separate and higher objects of design.

145. Thus, for instance, in the architecture which Niccola was occupied upon, when a boy, under his Byzantine master. Here is the door of the Baptistery at Pisa, again by Mr. Severn delightfully enlarged for us from a photograph. {1} The general idea of it is a square-headed opening in a solid wall, faced by an arch carried on shafts. And the ornament does indeed follow this construction so that the eye catches it with ease,—but under what arbitrary conditions! In the square door, certainly the side-posts of it are as important members as the lintel they carry; but the lintel is carved elaborately, and the side-posts left blank. Of the facing arch and shaft, it would be similarly difficult to say whether the sustaining vertical, or sustained curve, were the more important member of the construction; but the decorator now reverses the distribution of his care, adorns the vertical member with passionate elaboration, and runs a narrow band, of comparatively uninteresting work, round the arch. Between this outer shaft and inner door is a square pilaster, of which the architect carves one side, and lets the other alone. It is followed by a smaller shaft and arch, in which he reverses his treatment of the outer order by cutting the shaft delicately and the arch deeply. Again, whereas in what is called the decorated construction of English Gothic, the pillars would have been left plain and the spandrils deep cut,—here, are we to call it decoration of the construction, when the pillars are carved and the spandrils left plain? Or when, finally, either these spandril spaces on each side of the arch, or the corresponding slopes of the gable, are loaded with recumbent figures by the sculptors of the renaissance, are we to call, for instance, Michael Angelo's Dawn and Twilight, only the decorations of the sloping plinths of a tomb, or trace to a geometrical propriety the subsequent rule in

Italy that no window could be properly complete for living people to look out of, without having two stone people sitting on the corners of it above? I have heard of charming young ladies occasionally, at very crowded balls, sitting on the stairs,—would you call them, in that case, only decorations of the construction of the staircase?

{Footnote 1: Plate 5 is from the photograph itself; the enlarged drawing showed the arrangement of parts more clearly, but necessarily omitted detail which it is better here to retain.}

146. You will find, on consideration, the ultimate fact to be that to which I have just referred you;—my statement in "Aratra," that the idea of a construction originally useful is retained in good architecture, through all the amusement of its ornamentation; as the idea of the proper function of any piece of dress ought to be retained through its changes in form or embroidery. A good spire or porch retains the first idea of a roof usefully covering a space, as a Norman high cap or elongated Quaker's bonnet retains the original idea of a simple covering for the head; and any extravagance of subsequent fancy may be permitted, so long as the notion of use is not altogether lost. A girl begins by wearing a plain round hat to shade her from the sun; she ties it down over her ears on a windy day; presently she decorates the edge of it, so bent, with flowers in front, or the riband that ties it with a bouquet at the side, and it becomes a bonnet. This decorated construction may be discreetly changed, by endless fashion, so long as it does not become a clearly useless riband round the middle of the head, or a clearly useless saucer on the top of it.

147. Again, a Norman peasant may throw up the top of her cap into a peak, or a Bernese one put gauze wings at the side of it, and still be dressed with propriety, so long as her hair is modestly confined, and her ears healthily protected, by the matronly safeguard of the real construction. She ceases to be decorously dressed only when the material becomes too flimsy to answer such essential purpose, and the flaunting pendants or ribands can only answer the ends of coquetry or ostentation. Similarly, an architect may deepen or enlarge, in fantastic exaggeration, his original Westmoreland gable into Rouen porch, and his original square roof into Coventry spire; but he must not put within his splendid porch, a little door where two persons cannot together get in, nor cut his spire away into hollow filigree, and mere ornamental perviousness to wind and rain.

148. Returning to our door at Pisa, we shall find these general questions as to the distribution of ornament much confused with others as to its time and style. We are at once, for instance, brought to a pause as to the degree in which the ornamentation was once carried out in the doors themselves. Their surfaces were, however, I doubt not, once recipients of the most elaborate

ornament, as in the Baptistery of Florence; and in later bronze, by John of Bologna, in the door of the Pisan cathedral opposite this one. And when we examine the sculpture and placing of the lintel, which at first appeared the most completely Greek piece of construction of the whole, we find it so far advanced in many Gothic characters, that I once thought it a later interpolation cutting the inner pilasters underneath their capitals, while the three statues set on it are certainly, by several tens of years, later still.

149. How much ten years did at this time, one is apt to forget; and how irregularly the slower minds of the older men would surrender themselves, sadly, or awkwardly, to the vivacities of their pupils. The only wonder is that it should be usually so easy to assign conjectural dates within twenty or thirty years; but, at Pisa, the currents of tradition and invention run with such cross eddies, that I often find myself utterly at fault. In this lintel, for instance, there are two pieces separated by a narrower one, on which there has been an inscription, of which in my enlarged plate you may trace, though, I fear, not decipher, the few letters that remain. The uppermost of these stones is nearly pure in its Byzantine style; the lower, already semi-Gothic. Both are exquisite of their kind, and we will examine them closely; but first note these points about the stones of them. We are discussing work at latest of the thirteenth century. Our loss of the inscription is evidently owing to the action of the iron rivets which have been causelessly used at the two horizontal joints. There was nothing whatever in the construction to make these essential, and, but for this error, the entire piece of work, as delicate as an ivory tablet, would be as intelligible to-day as when it was laid in its place. {1}

{Footnote: Plates 6 and 7 give, in greater clearness, the sculpture of this lintel, for notes on which see Appendix.}

150. *Laid.* I pause upon this word, for it is an important one. And I must devote the rest of this lecture to consideration merely of what follows from the difference between laying a stone and setting it up, whether we regard sculpture or construction. The subject is so wide, I scarcely know how to approach it. Perhaps it will be the pleasantest way to begin if I read you a letter from one of yourselves to me. A very favourite pupil, who travels third class always, for sake of better company, wrote to me the other day: "One of my fellow-travellers, who was a builder, or else a master mason, told me that the way in which red sandstone buildings last depends entirely on the way in which the stone is laid. It must lie as it does in the quarry; but he said that very few workmen could always tell the difference between the joints of planes of cleavage and the—something else which I couldn't catch,—by which he meant, I suppose planes of stratification. He said too that some people, though they were very particular

{Illustration: PLATE VI.—THE STORY OF ST. JOHN. ADVENT.}

about having the stone laid well, allowed blocks to stand in the rain the wrong way up, and that they never recovered one wetting. The stone of the same quarry varies much, and he said that moss will grow immediately on good stone, but not on bad. How curious,—nature helping the best workman!" Thus far my favourite pupil.

151. 'Moss will grow on the best stone.' The first thing your modern restorer would do is to scrape it off; and with it, whatever knitted surface, half moss root, protects the interior stone. Have you ever considered the infinite functions of protection to mountain form exercised by the mosses and lichens? It will perhaps be refreshing to you after our work among the Pisan marbles and legends, if we have a lecture or two on moss. Meantime I need not tell you that it would not be a satisfactory natural arrangement if moss grew on marble, and that all fine workmanship in marble implies equal exquisiteness of surface and edge.

152. You will observe also that the importance of laying the stone in the building as it lay in its bed was from the first recognised by all good northern architects, to such extent that to lay stones 'en delit,' or in a position out of their bedding, is a recognized architectural term in France, where all structural building takes its rise; and in that form of 'delit' the word gets most curiously involved with the Latin delictum and deliquium. It would occupy the time of a whole lecture if I entered into the confused relations of the words derived from lectus, liquidus, delinquo, diliquo, and deliquesco; and of the still more confused, but beautifully confused, (and enriched by confusion,) forms of idea, whether respecting morality or marble, arising out of the meanings of these words: the notions of a bed gathered or strewn for the rest, whether of rocks or men; of the various states of solidity and liquidity connected with strength, or with repose; and of the duty of staying quiet in a place, or under a law, and the mischief of leaving it, being all fastened in the minds of early builders, and of the generations of men for whom they built, by the unescapable bearing of geological laws on their life; by the ease or difficulty of splitting rocks, by the variable consistency of the fragments split, by the innumerable questions occurring practically as to bedding and cleavage in every kind of stone, from tufo to granite, and by the unseemly, or beautiful, destructive, or protective, effects of decomposition. {1} The same processes of time which cause your Oxford oolite to flake away like the leaves of a mouldering book, only warm with a glow of perpetually deepening gold the marbles of Athens and Verona; and the same laws of chemical change which reduce the granites of Dartmoor to porcelain clay, bind the sands of Coventry into stones which can be built up halfway to the sky.

{Footnote 1: This passage cannot but seem to the reader loose and fantastic. I have elaborate notes, and many an unwritten thought, on these matters, but no time or strength to develop them. The passage is not fantastic, but the rapid index of what I know to be true in all the named particulars. But compare, for mere rough illustration of what I mean, the moral ideas relating to the stone of Jacob's pillow, or the tradition of it, with those to which French Flamboyant Gothic owes its character.}

153. But now, as to the matter immediately before us, observe what a double question arises about laying stones as they lie in the quarry. First, how *do* they lie in the quarry? Secondly, how can we lay them so in every part of our building?

A. How do they lie in the quarry? Level, perhaps, at Stonesfield and Coventry; but at an angle of 45° at Carrara; and for aught I know, of 90° in Paros or Pentelicus. Also, the *bedding* is of prime importance at Coventry, but the *cleavage* at Coniston. {1}

{Footnote 1: There are at least four definite cleavages at Coniston, besides joints. One of these cleavages furnishes the Coniston slate of commerce; another forms the ranges of Wetherlam and Yewdale crag; a third cuts these ranges to pieces, striking from north-west to south-east; and a fourth into other pieces, from north-east to south-west.}

B. And then, even if we know what the quarry bedding is, how are we to keep it always in our building? You may lay the stones of a wall carefully level, but how will you lay those of an arch? You think these, perhaps, trivial, or merely curious questions. So far from it, the fact that while the bedding in Normandy is level, that at Carrara is steep, and that the forces which raised the beds of Carrara crystallized them also, so that the cleavage which is all-important in the stones of my garden wall is of none in the duomo of Pisa,—simply determined the possibility of the existence of Pisan sculpture at all, and regulated the whole life and genius of Nicholas the Pisan and of Christian art. And, again, the fact that you can put stones in true bedding in a wall, but cannot in an arch, determines the structural transition from classical to Gothic architecture.

154. The *structural* transition, observe; only a part, and that not altogether a coincident part, of the *moral* transition. Read carefully, if you have time, the articles 'Pierre' and 'Meneau' in M. Violet le Duc's Dictionary of Architecture, and you will know everything that is of importance in the changes dependent on the mere qualities of *matter*. I must, however, try to set in your view also the relative acting qualities of *mind*.

You will find that M. Violet le Duc traces all the forms of Gothic tracery to the geometrical and practically serviceable development of the stone 'chassis,' chasing, or frame, for the glass. For instance, he attributes the use of the cusp or 'redent' in its more complex forms, to the necessity, or convenience, of diminishing the space of glass which the tracery grasps; and he attributes the reductions of the mouldings in the tracery bar under portions of one section, to the greater facility thus obtained by the architect in directing his workmen. The plan of a window once given, and the moulding-section,—all is said, thinks M. Violet le Duc. Very convenient indeed, for modern architects who have commission on the cost. But certainly not necessary, and perhaps even inconvenient, to Niccola Pisano, who is himself his workman, and cuts his own traceries, with his apron loaded with dust.

155. Again, the *re*dent—the 'tooth within tooth' of a French tracery—may be necessary, to bite its glass. But the cusp, cuspis, spiny or spearlike point of a thirteenth century illumination, is not in the least necessary to transfix the parchment. Yet do you suppose that the structural convenience of the redent entirely effaces from the mind of the designer the aesthetic characters which he seeks in the cusp? If you could for an instant imagine this, you would be undeceived by a glance either at the early redents of Amiens, fringing hollow vaults, or the late redents of Rouen, acting as crockets on the *outer* edges of pediments. 156. Again: if you think of the tracery in its *bars*, you call the cusp a redent; but if you think of it in the *openings*, you call the apertures of it foils. Do you suppose that the thirteenth century builder thought only of the strength of the bars of his enclosure, and never of the beauty of the form he enclosed? You will find in my chapter on the Aperture, in the "Stones of Venice," full development of the aesthetic laws relating to both these forms, while you may see, in Professor Willis's 'Architecture of the Middle Ages,' a beautiful analysis of the development of tracery from the juxtaposition of aperture; and in the article 'Meneau,' just quoted of M. Violet le Duc, an equally beautiful analysis of its development from the masonry of the chassis. You may at first think that Professor Willis's analysis is inconsistent with M. Violet le Duc's. But they are no more inconsistent than the accounts of the growth of a human being would be, if given by two anatomists, of whom one had examined only the skeleton and the other only the respiratory system; and who, therefore, supposed—the first, that the animal had been made only to leap, and the other only to sing. I don't mean that either of the writers I name are absolutely thus narrow in their own views, but that, so far as inconsistency appears to exist between them, it is of that partial kind only.

157. And for the understanding of our Pisan traceries we must introduce a third element of similarly distinctive nature. We must, to press our simile a little farther, examine the growth of the animal as if it had been made neither to leap, nor to sing, but only to think. We must observe the transitional states of its nerve power; that is to say, in our window tracery we must consider not merely how its ribs are built, (or how it stands,) nor merely how its openings

are shaped, or how it breathes; but also what its openings are made to light, or its shafts to receive, of picture or image. As the limbs of the building, it may be much; as the lungs of the building, more. As the *eyes* {1} of the building, what?

{Footnote 1: I am ashamed to italicize so many words; but these passages, written for oral delivery, can only be understood if read with oral emphasis. This is the first aeries of lectures which I have printed as they were to be spoken; and it is a great mistake.}

158. Thus you probably have a distinct idea—those of you at least who are interested in architecture—of the shape of the windows in Westminster Abbey, in the Cathedral of Chartres, or in the Duomo of Milan. Can any of you, I should like to know, make a guess at the shape of the windows in the Sistine Chapel, the Stanze of the Vatican, the Scuola di San Rocco, or the lower church of Assisi? The soul or anima of the first three buildings is in their windows; but of the last three, in their walls.

All these points I may for the present leave you to think over for yourselves, except one, to which I must ask yet for a few moments your further attention.

159. The trefoils to which I have called your attention in Niccola's pulpit are as absolutely without structural office in the circles as in the panels of the font beside it. But the circles are drawn with evident delight in the lovely circular line, while the trefoil is struck out by Niccola so roughly that there is not a true compass curve or section in any part of it.

Roughly, I say. Do you suppose I ought to have said carelessly? So far from it, that if one sharper line or more geometric curve had been given, it would have caught the eye too strongly, and drawn away the attention from the sculpture. But imagine the feeling with which a French master workman would first see these clumsy intersections of curves. It would be exactly the sensation with which a practical botanical draughtsman would look at a foliage background of Sir Joshua Reynolds.

But Sir Joshua's sketched leaves would indeed imply some unworkmanlike haste. We must not yet assume the Pisan master to have allowed himself in any such. His mouldings may be hastily cut, for they are, as I have just said, unnecessary to his structure, and disadvantageous to his decoration; but he is not likely to be careless about arrangements necessary for strength. His mouldings may be cut hastily, but do you think his *joints* will be?

160. What subject of extended inquiry have we in this word, ranging from the cementless clefts between the couchant stones of the walls of the kings of Rome, whose iron rivets you had but the other day placed in your hands by their discoverer, through the grip of the stones of the Tower of the Death-watch, to the subtle joints in the marble armour of the Florentine Baptistery!

Our own work must certainly be left with a rough surface at this place, and we will fit the edges of it to our next piece of study as closely as we may.

LECTURE VII.
MARBLE RAMPANT.

161. I closed my last lecture at the question respecting Nicholas's masonry. His mouldings may be careless, but do you think his joints will be?

I must remind you now of the expression as to the building of the communal palace—"of *dressed* stones" {1}—as opposed to the Tower of the Death-watch, in which the grip of cement had been so good. Virtually, you will find that the schools of structural architecture are those which use cement to bind

{Footnote 1: "Pietre conce." The portion of the has-reliefs of Orvieto, given in the opposite plate, will show the importance of the jointing. Observe the way in which the piece of stone with the three principal figures is dovetailed above the extended band, and again in the rise above the joint of the next stone on the right, the sculpture of the wings being carried across the junction. I have chosen this piece on purpose, because the loss of the broken fragment, probably broken by violence, and the only serious injury which the sculptures have received, serves to show the perfection of the uninjured surface, as compared with northern sculpture of the same date. I have thought it well to show at the same time the modern German engraving of the subject, respecting which see Appendix.}

{Illustration: PLATE VIII.—"THE CHARGE TO ADAM." GIOVANNI PISANO.}

their materials together, and in which, therefore, balance of *weight* becomes a continual and inevitable question. But the schools of sculptural architecture are those in which stones are fitted without cement, in which, therefore, the question of *fitting* or adjustment is continual and inevitable, but the sustainable weight practically unlimited.

162. You may consider the Tower of the Death-watch as having been knit together like the mass of a Roman brick wall.

But the dressed stone work of the thirteenth century is the hereditary completion of such block-laying, as the Parthenon in marble; or, in tufo, as that which was shown you so lately in the walls of Romulus; and the decoration of that system of couchant stone is by the finished grace of mosaic or sculpture.

163. It was also pointed out to you by Mr. Parker that there were two forms of Cyclopean architecture; one of level blocks, the other of polygonal,— contemporary, but in localities affording different material of stone.

I have placed in this frame examples of the Cyclopean horizontal, and the Cyclopean polygonal, architecture of the thirteenth century. And as Hubert of Lucca was the master of the new buildings at Florence, I have chosen the Cyclopean horizontal from his native city of Lucca; and as our Nicholas and John brought their new Gothic style into practice at Orvieto, I have chosen the Cyclopean polygonal from their adopted city of Orvieto.

Both these examples of architecture are early thirteenth century work, the beginnings of its new and Christian style, but beginnings with which Nicholas and John had nothing to do; they were part of the national work going on round them.

164. And this example from Lucca is of a very important class indeed. It is from above the east entrance gate of Lucca, which bears the cross above it, as the doors of a Christian city should. Such a city is, or ought to be, a place of peace, as much as any monastery.

This custom of placing the cross above the gate is Byzantine-Christian; and here are parallel instances of its treatment from Assisi. The lamb with the cross is given in the more elaborate arch of Verona.

165. But farther. The mosaic of this cross is so exquisitely fitted that no injury has been received by it to this day from wind or weather. And the horizontal dressed stones are laid so daintily that not an edge of them has stirred; and, both to draw your attention to their beautiful fitting, and as a substitute for cement, the architect cuts his uppermost block so as to dovetail into the course below.

Dovetail, I say deliberately. This is stone carpentry, in which the carpenter despises glue. I don't say he won't use glue, and glue of the best, but he feels it to be a nasty thing, and that it spoils his wood or marble. None, at least, he determines shall be seen outside, and his laying of stones shall be so solid and so adjusted that, take all the cement away, his wall shall yet stand.

Stonehenge, the Parthenon, the walls of the Kings, this gate of Lucca, this window of Orvieto, and this tomb at Verona, are all built on the Cyclopean principle. They will stand without cement, and no cement shall be seen outside. Mr. Burgess and I actually tried the experiment on this tomb. Mr. Burgess modelled every stone of it in clay, put them together, and it stood.

166. Now there are two most notable characteristics about this Cyclopean architecture to which I beg your close attention.

The first: that as the laying of stones is so beautiful, their joints become a subject of admiration, and great part of the architectural ornamentation is in the beauty of lines of separation, drawn as finely as possible. Thus the separating lines of the bricks at Siena, of this gate at Lucca, of the vault at Verona, of this window at Orvieto, and of the contemporary refectory at Furness Abbey, are a main source of the pleasure you have in the building.

Nay, they are not merely engravers' lines, but, in finest practice, they are mathematical lines—length without breadth. Here in my hand is a little shaft of Florentine mosaic executed at the present day. The separations between the stones are, in dimension, mathematical lines. And the two sides of the thirteenth century porch of St. Anastasia at Verona are built in this manner,—so exquisitely, that for some time, my mind not having been set at it, I passed them by as painted!

167. That is the first character of the Florentine Cyclopean But secondly; as the joints are so firm, and as the building must never stir or settle after it is built, the sculptor may trust his work to two stones set side by side, or one above another, and carve continuously over the whole surface, disregarding the joints, if he so chooses.

Of the degree of precision with which Nicholas of Pisa and his son adjusted their stones, you may judge by this rough sketch of a piece of St. Mary's of the Thorn, in which the design is of panels enclosing very delicately sculptured heads; and one would naturally suppose that the enclosing panels would be made of jointed pieces, and the heads carved separately and inserted. But the Pisans would have considered that unsafe masonry,—liable to the accident of the heads being dropped out, or taken away. John of Pisa did indeed use such masonry, of necessity, in his fountain; and the bas-reliefs *have* been taken away. But here one great block of marble forms part of two panels, and the mouldings and head are both carved in the solid, the joint running just behind the neck.

168. Such masonry is, indeed, supposing there were no fear of thieves, gratuitously precise in a case of this kind, in which the ornamentation is in separate masses, and might be separately carved. But when the ornamentation is current, and flows or climbs along the stone in the manner of waves or plants, the concealment of the joints of the pieces of marble becomes altogether essential. And here we enter upon a most curious group of associated characters in Gothic as opposed to Greek architecture.

169. If you have been able to read the article to which I referred you, 'Meneau,' in M. Violet le Duc's dictionary, you know that one great condition of the perfect Gothic structure is that the stones shall be 'en de-lit,' set up on end. The ornament then, which on the reposing or couchant stone was current only, on the erected stone begins to climb also, and becomes, in the most heraldic sense of the term, rampant.

In the heraldic sense, I say, as distinguished from the still wider original sense of advancing with a stealthy, creeping, or clinging motion, as a serpent on the ground, and a cat, or a vine, up a tree-stem. And there is one of these reptile, creeping, or rampant things, which is the first whose action was translated into marble, and otherwise is of boundless importance in the arts and labours of man.

170. You recollect Kingsley's expression,—now hackneyed, because admired for its precision,—the '*crawling foam*,' of waves advancing on sand. Tennyson has somewhere also used, with equal truth, the epithet 'climbing' of the spray of breakers against vertical rock. {1} In either instance, the sea action is literally 'rampant'; and the course of a great breaker, whether in its first proud likeness to a rearing horse, or in the humble and subdued gaining of the outmost verge of its foam on the sand, or the intermediate spiral whorl which gathers into a lustrous precision, like that of a polished shell, the grasping force of a giant, you have the most vivid sight and embodiment of literally rampant energy; which the Greeks expressed in their symbolic Poseidon, Scylla, and sea-horse, by the head and crest of the man, dog, or horse, with the body of the serpent; and of which you will find the slower image, in vegetation, rendered both by the spiral tendrils of grasping or climbing plants, and the perennial gaining of the foam or the lichen upon barren shores of stone.

{Footnote: Perhaps I am thinking of Lowell, not Tennyson; I have not time to look.}

171. If you will look to the thirtieth chapter of vol. i. in the new edition of the "Stones of Venice," which, by the gift of its publishers, I am enabled to lay on your table to be placed in your library, you will find one of my first and most eager statements of the necessity of inequality or change in form, made against the common misunderstanding of Greek symmetry, and illustrated by a woodcut of the spiral ornament on the treasury of Atreus at Mycenae. All that is said in that chapter respecting nature and the ideal, I now beg most earnestly to recommend and ratify to you; but although, even at that time, I knew more of Greek art than my antagonists, my broken reading has given me no conception of the range of its symbolic power, nor of the function of that more or less formal spiral line, as expressive, not only of the waves of the sea, but of the zones of the whirlpool, the return of the tempest, and the involution of the labyrinth. And although my readers say that I wrote then better than I write now, I cannot refer you to the passage without asking you to pardon in it what I now hold to be the petulance and vulgarity of expression, disgracing the importance of the truth it contains. A little while ago, without displeasure, you permitted me to delay you by the account of a dispute on a matter of taste between my father and me, in which he was quietly and unavailingly right. It seems to me scarcely a day, since, with boyish conceit, I resisted his wise entreaties that I would re-word this clause; and especially take out of it the description of a sea-wave as "laying a great white tablecloth of foam" all the way to the shore. Now, after an interval of twenty years, I refer you to the passage, repentant and humble as far as regards its

style, which people sometimes praised, but with absolue re-assertion of the truth and value of its contents, which people always denied. As natural form is varied, so must beautiful ornament be varied. You are not an artist by reproving nature into deathful sameness, but by animating your copy of her into vital variation. But I thought at that time that only Goths were rightly changeful. I never thought Greeks were. Their reserved variation escaped me, or I thought it accidental. Here, however, is a coin of the finest Greek workmanship, which shows you their mind in this matter unmistakably. Here are the waves of the Adriatic round a knight of Tarentum, and there is no doubt of their variableness.

172. This pattern of sea-wave, or river whirlpool, entirely sacred in the Greek mind, and the {Greek: *bostruchos*} or similarly curling wave in flowing hair, are the two main sources of the spiral form in lambent or rampant decoration. Of such lambent ornament, the most important piece is the crocket, of which I rapidly set before you the origin.

173. Here is a drawing of the gable of the bishop's throne in the upper church at Assisi, of the exact period when the mosaic workers of the thirteenth century at Rome adopted rudely the masonry of the north. Briefly, this is a Greek temple pediment, in which, doubtful of their power to carve figures beautiful enough, they cut a trefoiled hold for ornament, and bordered the edges with harlequinade of mosaic. They then call to their help the Greek sea-waves, and let the surf of the Ægean climb along the slopes, and toss itself at the top into a fleur-de-lys. Every wave is varied in outline and proportionate distance, though cut with a precision of curve like that of the sea itself. From this root we are able—but it must be in a lecture on crockets only—to trace the succeeding changes through the curl of Richard II.'s hair, and the crisp leaves of the forests of Picardy, to the knobbed extravagances of expiring Gothic. But I must to-day let you compare one piece of perfect Gothic work with the perfect Greek.

174. There is no question in my own mind, and, I believe, none in that of any other long-practised student of mediæval art, that in pure structural Gothic the church of St. Urbain at Troyes is without rival in Europe. Here is a rude sketch of its use of the crocket in the spandrils of its external tracery, and here are the waves of the Greek sea round the son of Poseidon. Seventeen hundred years are between them, but the same mind is in both. I wonder how many times seventeen hundred years Mr. Darwin will ask, to retrace the Greek designer of this into his primitive ape; or how many times six hundred years of such improvements as we have made on the church of St. Urbain, will be needed in order to enable our descendants to regard the designers of that, as only primitive apes.

175. I return for a moment to my gable at Assisi. You see that the crest of the waves at the top form a rude likeness of a fleur-de-lys. There is, however, in this form no real intention of imitating a flower, any more than in the meeting of the tails of these two Etruscan griffins. The notable circumstance in this piece of Gothic is its advanced form of crocket, and its prominent foliation, with nothing in the least approaching to floral ornament.

176. And now, observe this very curious fact in the personal character of two contemporary artists. See the use of my manually graspable flag. Here is John of Pisa,—here Giotto. They are contemporary for twenty years;—but these are the prime of Giotto's life, and the last of John's life: virtually, Giotto is the later workman by full twenty years.

But Giotto always uses severe geometrical mouldings, and disdains all luxuriance of leafage to set off interior sculpture.

John of Pisa not only adopts Gothic tracery, but first allows himself enthusiastic use of rampant vegetation;—and here in the façade of Orvieto, you have not only perfect Gothic in the sentiment of Scripture history, but such luxurious ivy ornamentation as you cannot afterwards match for two hundred years. Nay, you can scarcely match it then—for grace of line, only in the richest flamboyant of France.

177. Now this fact would set you, if you looked at art from its aesthetic side only, at once to find out what German artists had taught Giovanni Pisano. There *were* Germans teaching him,—some teaching him many things; and the intense conceit of the modern German artist imagines them to have taught him all things.

But he learnt his luxuriance, and Giotto his severity, in another school. The quality in both is Greek; and altogether moral. The grace and the redundance of Giovanui are the first strong manifestation of those characters in the Italian mind which culminate in the Madonnas of Luini and the arabesques of Raphael. The severity of Giotto belongs to him, on the contrary, not only as one of the strongest practical men who ever lived on this solid earth, but as the purest and firmest reformer of the discipline of the Christian Church, of whose writings any remains exist.

178. Of whose writings, I say; and you look up, as doubtful that he has left any. Hieroglyphics, then, let me say instead; or, more accurately still, hierographics. St. Francis, in what he wrote and said, taught much that was false. But Giotto, his true disciple, nothing but what was true. And where *he* uses an arabesque of foliage, depend upon it it will be to purpose—not redundant. I return for the time to our soft and luxuriant John of Pisa.

179. Soft, but with no unmanly softness; luxuriant, but with no unmannered luxury. To him you owe as to their first sire in art, the grace of Ghiberti, the

tenderness of Raphael, the awe of Michael Angelo. Second-rate qualities in all the three, but precious in their kind, and learned, as you shall see, essentially from this man. Second-rate he also, but with most notable gifts of this inferior kind. He is the Canova of the thirteenth century; but the Canova of the thirteenth, remember, was necessarily a very different person from the Canova of the eighteenth.

The Cauova of the eighteenth century mimicked Greek grace for the delight of modern revolutionary sensualists. The Canova of the thirteenth century brought living Gothic truth into the living faith of his own time.

Greek truth, and Gothic 'liberty,'—in that noble sense of the word, derived from the Latin 'liber,' of which I have already spoken, and which in my next lecture I will endeavour completely to develope. Meanwhile let me show you, as far as I can, the architecture itself about which these subtle questions arise.

180. Here are five frames, containing the best representations I can get for you of the façade of the cathedral of Orvieto. I must remind you, before I let you look at them, of the reason why that cathedral was built; for I have at last got to the end of the parenthesis which began in my second lecture, on the occasion of our hearing that John of Pisa was sent for to Perugia, to carve the tomb of Pope Urban IV.; and we must now know who this Pope was.

181. He was a Frenchman, born at that Troyes, in Champagne, which I gave you as the centre of French architectural skill, and Royalist character. He was born in the lowest class of the people, rose like Wolsey; became Bishop of Verdun; then, Patriarch of Jerusalem; returned in the year 1261, from his Patriarchate, to solicit the aid of the then Pope, Alexander IV., against the Saracen. I do not know on what day he arrived in Rome; but on the 25th of May, Alexander died, and the Cardinals, after three months' disputing, elected the suppliant Patriarch to be Pope himself.

182. A man with all the fire of France in him, all the faith, and all the insolence; incapable of doubting a single article of his creed, or relaxing one tittle of his authority; destitute alike of reason and of pity; and absolutely merciless either to an infidel, or an enemy. The young Prince Manfred, bastard son of Frederick II., now representing the main power of the German empire, was both; and against him the Pope brought into Italy a religious French knight, of character absolutely like his own, Charles of Anjou.

183. The young Manfred, now about twenty years old, was as good a soldier as he was a bad Christian; and there was no safety for Urban at Rome. The Pope seated himself on a worthy throne for a thirteenth-century St. Peter. Fancy the rock of Edinburgh Castle, as steep on all sides as it is to the west; and as long as the Old Town; and you have the rock of Orvieto.

184. Here, enthroned against the gates of hell, in unassailable fortitude, and unfaltering faith, sat Urban; the righteousness of his cause presently to be avouched by miracle, notablest among those of the Roman Church. Twelve miles east of his rock, beyond the range of low Apennine, shone the quiet lake, the Loch Leven of Italy, from whose island the daughter of Theodoric needed not to escape—Fate seeking her there; and in a little chapel on its shore a Bohemian priest, infected with Northern infidelity, was brought back to his allegiance by seeing the blood drop from the wafer in his hand. And the Catholic Church recorded this heavenly testimony to her chief mystery, in the Festa of the Corpus Domini, and the Fabric of Orvieto.

185. And sending was made for John, and for all good labourers in marble; but Urban never saw a stone of the great cathedral laid. His citation of Manfred to appear in his presence to answer for his heresy, was fixed against the posts of the doors of the old Duomo. But Urban had dug the foundation of the pile to purpose, and when he died at Perugia, still breathed, from his grave, calamity to Manfred, and made from it glory to the Church. He had secured the election of a French successor; from the rock of Orvieto the spirit of Urban led the French chivalry, when Charles of Anjou saw the day of battle come, so long desired. Manfred's Saracens, with their arrows, broke his first line; the Pope's legate blessed the second, and gave them absolution of all their sins, for their service to the Church. They charged for Orvieto with their old cry of 'Mont-Joie, Chevaliers!' and before night, while Urban lay sleeping in his carved tomb at Perugia, the body of Manfred lay only recognizable by those who loved him, naked among the slain.

186. Time wore on and on. The Suabian power ceased in Italy; between white and red there was now no more contest;—the matron of the Church, scarlet-robed, reigned, ruthless, on her seven hills. Time wore on; and, a hundred years later, now no more the power of the kings, but the power of the people,—rose against her. St. Michael, from the corn market,—Or San Michele,—the commercial strength of Florence, on a question of free trade in corn. And note, for a little bye piece of botany, that in Val d'Arno lilies grow among the corn instead of poppies. The purple gladiolus glows through all its green fields in early spring.

187. A question of free trade in corn, then, arose between Florence and Rome. The Pope's legate in Bologna stopped the supply of polenta, the Florentines depending on that to eat with their own oil. Very wicked, you think, of the Pope's legate, acting thus against quasi-Protestant Florence? Yes; just as wicked as the—not quasi-Protestants—but intensely positive Protestants, of Zurich, who tried to convert the Catholic forest-cantons by refusing them salt. Christendom has been greatly troubled about bread and salt: the then Protestant Pope, Zuinglius, was killed at the battle of Keppel, and the Catholic cantons therefore remain Catholic to this day; while the

consequences of this piece of protectionist economy at Bologna are equally interesting and direct.

188. The legate of Bologna, not content with stopping the supplies of maize to Florence, sent our own John Hawkwood, on the 24th June, 1375, to burn all the maize the Florentines had got growing; and the abbot of Montemaggiore sent a troop of Perugian religious gentlemen-riders to ravage similarly the territory of Siena. Whereupon, at Florence, the Gonfalonier of Justice, Aloesio Aldobrandini, rose in the Council of Ancients and proposed, as an enterprise worthy of Florentine generosity, the freedom of all the peoples who groaned under the tyranny of the Church. And Florence, Siena, Pisa, Lucca, and Arezzo,—all the great cities of Etruria, the root of religion in Italy,—joined against the tyranny of religion. Strangely, this Etrurian league is not now to restore Tarquin to Rome, but to drive the Roman Tarquin into exile. The story of Lucretia had been repeated in Perugia; but the Umbrian Lucretia had died, not by suicide, but by falling on the pavement from the window through which she tried to escape. And the Umbrian Sextus was the Abbot of Montemaggiore's nephew.

189. Florence raised her fleur-de-lys standard: and, in ten days, eighty cities of Romagua were free, out of the number of whose names I will read you only these—Urbino, Foligno, Spoleto, Narni, Camerino, Toscanella, Perugia, Orvieto.

And while the wind and the rain still beat the body of Manfred, by the shores of the Rio Verde, the body of Pope Urban was torn from its tomb, and not one stone of the carved work thereof left upon another. 190. I will only ask you to-day to notice farther that the Captain of Florence, in this war, was a 'Conrad of Suabia,' and that she gave him, beside her own flag, one with only the word 'Libertas' inscribed on it.

I told you that the first stroke of the bell on the Tower of the Lion began the carillon for European civil and religious liberty. But perhaps, even in the fourteenth century, Florence did not understand, by that word, altogether the same policy which is now preached in France, Italy, and England.

What she did understand by it, we will try to ascertain in the course of next lecture.

LECTURE VIII.
FRANCHISE.

191. In my first lecture of this course, you remember that I showed
you the Lion of St. Mark's with Niccola Pisano's, calling the one
an evangelical-preacher lion, and the other a real, and naturally
affectionate, lioness.

And the one I showed you as Byzantine, the other as Gothic.

So that I thus called the Greek art pious, and the Gothic profane.

Whereas in nearly all our ordinary modes of thought, and in all my own general references to either art, we assume Greek or classic work to be profane, and Gothic, pious, or religious.

192. Very short reflection, if steady and clear, will both show you how confused our ideas are usually on this subject, and how definite they may within certain limits become.

First of all, don't confuse piety with Christianity. There are pious Greeks and impious Greeks; pious Turks and impious Turks; pious Christians and impious Christians; pious modern infidels and impious modern infidels. In case you do not quite know what piety really means, we will try to know better in next lecture; for the present, understand that I mean distinctly to call Greek art, in the true sense of the word, pious, and Gothic, as opposed to it, profane.

193. But when I oppose these two words, Gothic and Greek, don't run away with the notion that I necessarily mean to oppose *Christian* and Greek. You must not confuse Gothic blood in a man's veins, with Christian feeling in a man's breast. There are unconverted and converted Goths; unconverted and converted Greeks. The Greek and Gothic temper is equally opposed, where the name of Christ has never been uttered by either, or when every other name is equally detested by both.

I want you to-day to examine with me that essential difference between Greek and Gothic temper, irrespective of creed, to which I have referred in my preface to the last edition of the "Stones of Venice," saying that the Byzantines gave law to Norman license. And I must therefore ask your patience while I clear your minds from some too prevalent errors as to the meaning of those two words, law and license.

194. There is perhaps no more curious proof of the disorder which impatient and impertinent science is introducing into classical thought and language,

than the title chosen by the Duke of Argyll for his interesting study of Natural History—'The Reign of Law.' Law cannot reign. If a natural law, it admits no disobedience, and has nothing to put right. If a human one, it can compel no obedience, and has no power to prevent wrong. A king only can reign;—a person, that is to say, who, conscious of natural law, enforces human law so far as it is just.

195. Kinghood is equally necessary in Greek dynasty, and in Gothic. Theseus is every inch a king, as well as Edward III. But the laws which they have to enforce on their own and their companions' humanity are opposed to each other as much as their dispositions are.

The function of a Greek king was to enforce labour.

That of a Gothic king, to restrain rage.

The laws of Greece determine the wise methods of labour; and the laws of France determine the wise restraints of passion.

For the sins of Greece are in Indolence, and its pleasures; and the sins of France are in fury, and its pleasures.

196. You are now again surprised, probably, at hearing me oppose France typically to Greece. More strictly, I might oppose only a part of France,—Normandy. But it is better to say, France, {1} as embracing the seat of the established Norman power in the Island of our Lady; and the province in which it was crowned,—Champagne.

{Footnote 1: "Normandie, la franche." "France, la solue;" (chanson de Roland). One of my good pupils referred me to this ancient and glorious French song.}

France is everlastingly, by birth, name, and nature, the country of the Franks, or free persons; and the first source of European frankness, or franchise. The Latin for franchise is libertas. But the modern or Cockney-English word liberty,—Mr. John Stuart Mill's,—is not the equivalent of libertas; and the modern or Cockney-French word liberté,—M. Victor Hugo's,—is not the equivalent of franchise.

197. The Latin for franchise, I have said, is libertas; the Greek is {Greek: *eleupheria*}. In the thoughts of all three nations, the idea is precisely the same, and the word used for the idea by each nation therefore accurately translates the word of the other: {Greek: *eleupheria*}—libertas—franchise—reciprocally translate each other. Leonidas is characteristically {Greek: *eleupheros*} among Greeks; Publicola, characteristically liber, among Romans; Edward III. and the Black Prince, characteristically frank among French. And that common idea, which the words express, as all the careful scholars among you will know, is, with all the three nations, mainly of

deliverance from the slavery of passion. To be {Greek: *eleupheros*}, liber, or franc, is first to have learned how to rule our own passions; and then, certain that our own conduct is right, to persist in that conduct against all resistance, whether of counter-opinion, counter pain, or counter-pleasure. To be defiant alike of the mob's thought, of the adversary's threat, and the harlot's temptation,—this is in the meaning of every great nation to be free; and the one condition upon which that freedom can be obtained is pronounced to you in a single verse of the 119th Psalm, "I will walk at liberty, for I seek Thy precepts."

198. Thy precepts:—Law, observe, being dominant over the Gothic as over the Greek king, but a quite different law. Edward III. feeling no anger against the Sieur de Ribaumont, and crowning him with his own pearl chaplet, is obeying the law of love, *restraining* anger; but Theseus, slaying the Minotaur, is obeying the law of justice, and *enforcing* anger.

The one is acting under the law of the charity, {Greek: *charis*} or grace of God; the other under the law of His judgment. The two together fulfil His {Greek: *krisis*} and {Greek: *agapae*}.

199. Therefore the Greek dynasties are finally expressed in the kinghoods of Minos, Rhadamanthus, and Aeacus, who judge infallibly, and divide arithmetically. But the dynasty of the Gothic king is in equity and compassion, and his arithmetic is in largesse,

> "*Whose moste joy was, I wis,*
>
> *When that she gave, and said, Have this.*"

So that, to put it in shortest terms of all, Greek law is of Stasy, and Gothic of Ecstasy; there is no limit to the freedom of the Gothic hand or heart, and the children are most in the delight and the glory of liberty when they most seek their Father's precepts.

200. The two lines I have just quoted are, as you probably remember, from Chaucer's translation of the French Romance of the Rose, out of which I before quoted to you the description of the virtue of Debonnaireté. Now that Debonnaireté of the Painted Chamber of Westminster is the typical figure used by the French sculptors and painters for 'franchise,' frankness, or Frenchness; but in the Painted Chamber, Debonnaireté, high breeding, 'out of goodnestedness,' or gentleness, is used, as an English king's English, of the Norman franchise. Here, then, is our own royalty,—let us call it Englishness, the grace of our proper kinghood;—and here is French royalty, the grace of French kinghood—Frenchness, rudely but sufficiently drawn by M. Didron from the porch of Chartres. She has the crown of fleur-de-lys, and William the Norman's shield.

201. Now this grace of high birth, the grace of his or her Most Gracious Majesty, has her name at Chartres written beside her, in Latin. Had it been in Greek, it would have been {Greek: *elevtheria*}. Being in Latin, what do you think it must be necessarily?—Of course, Libertas. Now M. Didron is quite the best writer on art that I know,—full of sense and intelligence; but of course, as a modern Frenchman,—one of a nation for whom the Latin and Gothic ideas of libertas have entirely vanished,—he is not on his guard against the trap here laid for him. He looks at the word libertas through his spectacles;—can't understand, being a thoroughly good antiquary, {1} how such a virtue, or privilege, could honestly be carved with approval in the twelfth century;—rubs his spectacles; rubs the inscription, to make sure of its every letter; stamps it, to make surer still;—and at last, though in a greatly bewildered state of mind, remains convinced that here is a sculpture of 'La Liberte' in the twelfth century. "C'est bien la liberte!" "On lit parfaitement libertas."

{Footnote 1: Historical antiquary; not art-antiquary I must limitedly say, however. He has made a grotesque mess of his account of the Ducal Palace of Venice, through his ignorance of the technical characters of sculpture.}

202. Not so, my good M. Didron!—a very different personage, this; of whom more, presently, though the letters of her name are indeed so plainly, 'Libertas, at non liberalitas,' liberalitas being the Latin for largesse, not for franchise.

This, then, is the opposition between the Greek and Gothic dynasties, in their passionate or vital nature; in the *animal* and *inbred* part of them;—Classic and romantic, Static and exstatic. But now, what opposition is there between their divine natures? Between Theseus and Edward III., as warriors, we now know the difference; but between Theseus and Edward III, as theologians; as dreaming and discerning creatures, as didactic kings,—engraving letters with the point of the sword, instead of thrusting men through with it,—changing the club into the ferula, and becoming schoolmasters as well as kings; what is, thus, the difference between them?

Theologians I called them. Philologians would be a better word,—lovers of the {Greek: *Logos*}, or Word, by which the heavens and earth were made. What logos, *about* this Logos, have they learned, or can they teach?

203. I showed you, in my first lecture, the Byzantine Greek lion, as descended by true unblemished line from the Nemean Greek; but with this difference: Heracles kills the beast, and makes a helmet and cloak of his skin; the Greek St. Mark converts the beast, and makes an evangelist of him.

Is not that a greater difference, think you, than one of mere decadence?

This 'maniera goffa e sproporzionata' of Vasari is not, then, merely the wasting away of former leonine strength into thin rigidities of death? There is another change going on at the same time,—body perhaps subjecting itself to spirit.

I will not teaze you with farther questions. The facts are simple enough. Theseus and Heracles have their religion, sincere and sufficient,—a religion of lion-killers, minotaur-killers, very curious and rude; Eleusinian mystery mingled in it, inscrutable to us now,—partly always so, even to them.

204. Well; the Greek nation, in process of time, loses its manliness,— becomes Graeculus instead of Greek. But though effeminate and feeble, it inherits all the subtlety of its art, all the cunning of its mystery; and it is converted to a more spiritual religion. Nor is it altogether degraded, even by the diminution of its animal energy. Certain spiritual phenomena are possible to the weak, which are hidden from the strong;—nay, the monk may, in his order of being, possess strength denied to the warrior. Is it altogether, think you, by blundering, or by disproportion in intellect or in body, that Theseus becomes St. Athanase? For that is the kind of change which takes place, from the days of the great King of Athens, to those of the great Bishop of Alexandria, in the thought and theology, or, summarily, in the spirit of the Greek.

Now we have learned indeed the difference between the Gothic knight and the Greek knight; but what will be the difference between the Gothic saint and Greek saint?

Franchise of body against constancy of body.

Franchise of thought, then, against constancy of thought.

Edward III. against Theseus.

And the Frank of Assisi against St. Athanase.

205. Utter franchise, utter gentleness in theological thought. Instead of, 'This is the faith, which except a man believe faithfully, he cannot be saved,' 'This is the love, which if a bird or an insect keep faithfully, it shall be saved.'

Gentlemen, you have at present arrived at a phase of natural science in which, rejecting alike the theology of the Byzantine, and the affection of the Frank, you can only contemplate a bird as flying under the reign of law, and a cricket as singing under the compulsion of caloric.

I do not know whether you yet feel that the position of your boat on the river also depends entirely on the reign of law, or whether, as your churches and concert-rooms are privileged in the possession of organs blown by steam, you are learning yourselves to sing by gas, and expect the Dies Irae to the announced by a steam-trumpet. But I can very positively assure you that, in my poor domain of imitative art, not all the mechanical or gaseous forces of the world, nor all the laws of the universe, will enable you either to see a colour, or draw a line, without that singular force anciently called the soul, which it was the function of the Greek to discipline in the duty of the servants of God, and of the Goth to lead into the liberty of His children.

206. But in one respect I wish you were more conscious of the existence of law than you appear to be. The difference which I have pointed out to you as existing between these great nations, exists also between two orders of intelligence among men, of which the one is usually called Classic, the other Romantic. Without entering into any of the fine distinctions between these two sects, this broad one is to be observed as constant: that the writers and painters of the Classic school set down nothing but what is known to be true, and set it down in the perfectest manner possible in their way, and are thenceforward authorities from whom there is no appeal. Romantic writers and painters, on the contrary, express themselves under the impulse of passions which may indeed lead them to the discovery of new truths, or to the more delightful arrangement or presentment of things already known: but their work, however brilliant or lovely, remains imperfect, and without authority. It is not possible, of course, to separate these two orders of men trenchantly: a classic writer may sometimes, whatever his care, admit an error, and a romantic one may reach perfection through enthusiasm. But, practically, you may separate the two for your study and your education; and, during your youth, the business of us your masters is to enforce on you the reading, for school work, only of classical books: and to see that your minds are both informed of the indisputable facts they contain, and accustomed to act with the infallible accuracy of which they set the example.

207. I have not time to make the calculation, but I suppose that the daily literature by which we now are principally nourished, is so large in issue that though St. John's "even the world itself could not contain the books which should be written" may be still hyperbole, it is nevertheless literally true that the world might be *wrapped* in the books which are written; and that the sheets of paper covered with type on any given subject, interesting to the modern mind, (say the prospects of the Claimant,) issued in the form of English morning papers during a single year, would be enough literally to pack the world in.

208. Now I will read you fifty-two lines of a classical author, which, once well read and understood, contain more truth than has been told you all this year by this whole globe's compass of print.

Fifty-two lines, of which you will recognize some as hackneyed, and see little to admire in others. But it is not possible to put the statements they contain into better English, nor to invalidate one syllable of the statements they contain. {1}

{Footnote 1: 'The Deserted Village,' line 251 to 302.}

209. Even those, and there may be many here, who would dispute the truth of the passage, will admit its exquisite distinctness and construction. If it be untrue, that is merely because I have not been taught by my modern education to recognize a classical author; but whatever my mistakes, or yours, may be, there *are* certain truths long known to all rational men, and indisputable. You may add to them, but you cannot diminish them. And it is the business of a University to determine what books of this kind exist, and to enforce the understanding of them.

210. The classical and romantic arts which we have now under examination therefore consist,—the first, in that which represented, under whatever symbols, truths respecting the history of men, which it is proper that all should know; while the second owes its interest to passionate impulse or incident. This distinction holds in all ages, but the distinction between the franchise of Northern, and the constancy of Byzantine, art, depends partly on the unsystematic play of emotion in the one, and the appointed sequence of known fact or determined judgment in the other.

You will find in the beginning of M. Didron's book, already quoted, an admirable analysis of what may be called the classic sequence of Christian theology, as written in the sculpture of the Cathedral of Chartres. You will find in the treatment of the façade of Orvieto the beginning of the development of passionate romance,—the one being grave sermon writing; the other, cheerful romance or novel writing: so that the one requires you to think, the other only to feel or perceive; the one is always a parable with a meaning, the other only a story with an impression.

211. And here I get at a result concerning Greek art, which is very sweeping and wide indeed. That it is all parable, but Gothic, as distinct from it, literal. So absolutely does this hold, that it reaches down to our modern school of landscape. You know I have always told you Turner belonged to the Greek school. Precisely as the stream of blood coming from under the throne of judgment in the Byzantine mosaic of Torcello is a sign of condemnation, his scarlet clouds are used by Turner as a sign of death; and just as on an Egyptian tomb the genius of death lays the sun down behind the horizon, so in his Cephalus and Procris, the last rays of the sun withdraw from the forest as the nymph expires.

And yet, observe, both the classic and romantic teaching may be equally earnest, only different in manner. But from classic art, unless you understand it, you may get nothing; from romantic art, even if you don't understand it, you get at least delight.

212. I cannot show the difference more completely or fortunately than by comparing Sir Walter Scott's type of libertas, with the franchise of Chartres Cathedral, or Debonnaireté of the Painted Chamber.

At Chartres, and Westminster, the high birth is shown by the crown; the strong bright life by the flowing hair; the fortitude by the conqueror's shield; and the truth by the bright openness of the face:

> *"She was not brown, nor dull of hue,*
>
> *But white as snowe, fallen newe."*

All these are symbols, which, if you cannot read, the image is to you only an uninteresting stiff figure. But Sir Walter's Franchise, Diana Vernon, interests you at once in personal aspect and character. She is no symbol to you; but if you acquaint yourself with her perfectly, you find her utter frankness, governed by a superb self-command; her spotless truth, refined by tenderness; her fiery enthusiasm, subdued by dignity; and her fearless liberty, incapable of doing wrong, joining to fulfil to you, in sight and presence, what the Greek could only teach by signs.

213. I have before noticed—though I am not sure that you have yet believed my statement of it—the significance of Sir Walter's as of Shakspeare's names; Diana 'Vernon, semper viret,' gives you the conditions of purity and youthful strength or spring which imply the highest state of libertas. By corruption of the idea of purity, you get the modern heroines of London Journal—or perhaps we may more fitly call it 'Cockney-daily'—literature. You have one of them in perfection, for instance, in Mr. Charles Reade's 'Griffith Gaunt'— "Lithe, and vigorous, and one with her great white gelding;" and liable to be entirely changed in her mind about the destinies of her life by a quarter of an hour's conversation with a gentleman unexpectedly handsome; the hero also being a person who looks at people whom he dislikes, with eyes "like a dog's in the dark;" and both hero and heroine having souls and intellects also precisely corresponding to those of a dog's in the dark, which is indeed the essential picture of the practical English national mind at this moment,— happy if it remains doggish,—Circe not usually being content with changing people into dogs only. For the Diana Vernon of the Greek is Artemis Laphria, who is friendly to the dog; not to the swine. Do you see, by the way, how perfectly the image is carried out by Sir Walter in putting his Diana on the border country? "Yonder blue hill is in Scotland," she says to her cousin,—not in the least thinking less of him for having been concerned, it may be, in one of Bob Roy's forays. And so gradually you get the idea of Norman franchise carried out in the free-rider or free-booter; not safe from

degradation on that side also; but by no means of swinish temper, or foraging, as at present the British speculative public, only with the snout.

214. Finally, in the most soft and domestic form of virtue, you have Wordsworth's ideal:

> *"Her household motions light and free,*
>
> *And steps of virgin liberty."*

The distinction between these northern types of feminine virtue, and the figures of Alcestis, Antigone, or Iphigenia, lies deep in the spirit of the art of either country, and is carried out into its most unimportant details. We shall find in the central art of Florence at once the thoughtfulness of Greece and the gladness of England, associated under images of monastic severity peculiar to herself.

And what Diana Vernon is to a French ballerine dancing the Cancan, the 'libertas' of Chartres and Westminster is to the 'liberty' of M. Victor Hugo and Mr. John Stuart Mill.

LECTURE IX.
THE TYRRHENE SEA.

215. We may now return to the points of necessary history, having our ideas fixed within accurate limits as to the meaning of the word Liberty; and as to the relation of the passions which separated the Guelph and Ghibelline to those of our own days.

The Lombard or Guelph league consisted, after the accession of Florence, essentially of the three great cities—Milan, Bologna, and Florence; the Imperial or Ghibelline league, of Verona, Pisa, and Siena. Venice and Genoa, both nominally Guelph, are in furious contention always for sea empire while Pisa and Genoa are in contention, not so much for empire, as honour. Whether the trade of the East was to go up the Adriatic, or round by the Gulf of Genoa, was essentially a mercantile question; but whether, of the two ports in sight of each other, Pisa or Genoa was to be the Queen of the Tyrrhene Sea, was no less distinctly a personal one than which of two rival beauties shall preside at a tournament.

216. This personal rivalry, so far as it was separated from their commercial interests, was indeed mortal, but not malignant. The quarrel was to be decided to the death, but decided with honour; and each city had four observers permittedly resident in the other, to give account of all that was done there in naval invention and armament.

217. Observe, also, in the year 1251, when we quitted our history, we left Florence not only Guelph, as against the Imperial power, (that is to say, the body of her knights who favoured the Pope and Italians, in dominion over those who favoured Manfred and the Germans), but we left her also definitely with her apron thrown over her shield; and the tradesmen and craftsmen in authority over the knight, whether German or Italian, Papal or Imperial.

That is in 1251. Now in these last two lectures I must try to mark the gist of the history of the next thirty years. The Thirty Years' War, this, of the middle ages, infinitely important to all ages; first observe, between Guelph and Ghibelline, ending in the humiliation of the Ghibelline; and, secondly, between Shield and Apron, or, if you like better, between Spear and Hammer, ending in the breaking of the Spear.

218. The first decision of battle, I say, is that between Guelph and Ghibelline, headed by two men of precisely oppposite characters, Charles of Anjou and Manfred of Suabia. That I may be able to define the opposition of their characters intelligibly, I must first ask your attention to some points of general scholarship. I said in my last lecture that, in this one, it would be

needful for us to consider what piety was, if we happened not to know; or worse than that, it may be, not instinctively to feel. Such want of feeling is indeed not likely in you, being English-bred; yet as it is the modern cant to consider all such sentiment as useless, or even shameful, we shall be in several ways advantaged by some examination of its nature. Of all classical writers, Horace is the one with whom English gentlemen have on the average most sympathy; and I believe, therefore, we shall most simply and easily get at our point by examining the piety of Horace.

219. You are perhaps, for the moment, surprised, whatever might have been admitted of Æneas, to hear Horace spoken of as a pious person. But of course when your attention is turned to the matter you will recollect many lines in which the word 'pietas' occurs, of which you have only hitherto failed to allow the force because you supposed Horace did not mean what he said.

220. But Horace always and altogether means what he says. It is just because—whatever his faults may have been—he was not a hypocrite, that English gentlemen are so fond of him. "Here is a frank fellow, anyhow," they say, "and a witty one." Wise men know that he is also wise. True men know that he is also true. But pious men, for want of attention, do not always know that he is pious.

One great obstacle to your understanding of him is your having been forced to construct Latin verses, with introduction of the word 'Jupiter' always, at need, when you were at a loss for a dactyl. You always feel as if Horace only used it also when he wanted a dactyl.

221. Get quit of that notion wholly. All immortal writers speak out of their hearts. Horace spoke out of the abundance of his heart, and tells you precisely what he is, as frankly as Montaigne. Note then, first, how modest he is: "Ne parva Tyrrhenum per aequor, vela darem;—Operosa parvus, carmina fingo." Trust him in such words; he absolutely means them; knows thoroughly that he cannot sail the Tyrrhene Sea,—knows that he cannot float on the winds of Matinum,—can only murmur in the sunny hollows of it among the heath.

But note, secondly, his pride: "Exegi monumentum sere perennius." He is not the least afraid to say that. He did it; knew he had done it; said he had done it; and feared no charge of arrogance.

222. Note thirdly, then, his piety, and accept his assured speech of it: "Dis pietas mea, et Musa, cordi est." He is perfectly certain of that also; serenely tells you so; and you had better believe him. Well for you, if you can believe him; for to believe him, you must understand him first; and I can tell you, you won't arrive at that understanding by looking out the word 'pietas' in your White-and-Riddle. If you do you will find those tiresome contractions,

Etym. Dub., stop your inquiry very briefly, as you go back; if you go forward, through the Italian pieta, you will arrive presently in another group of ideas, and end in misericordia, mercy, and pity. You must not depend on the form of the word; you must find out what it stands for in Horace's mind, and in Virgil's. More than race to the Roman; more than power to the statesman; yet helpless beside the grave,—"Non, Torquate, genus, non te facundia, non te, Restitvet pietas."

Nay, also what it stands for as an attribute, not only of men, but of gods; nor of those only as merciful, but also as avenging. Against Æneas himself, Dido invokes the waves of the Tyrrhene Sea, "si quid pia numina possunt." Be assured there is no getting at the matter by dictionary or context. To know what love means, you must love; to know what piety means, you must be pious.

223. Perhaps you dislike the word, now, from its vulgar use. You may have another if you choose, a metaphorical one,—close enough it seems to Christianity, and yet still absolutely distinct from it,—{Greek: *christos*}. Suppose, as you watch the white bloom of the olives of Val d'Arno and Val di Nievole, which modern piety and economy suppose were grown by God only to supply you with fine Lucca oil, you were to consider, instead, what answer you could make to the Socratio question, {Greek: *pothen un tis tovto to chrisma labot*}. {1}

{Footnote 1: Xem. Conviv., ii.}

224. I spoke to you first of Horace's modesty. All piety begins in modesty. You must feel that you are a very little creature, and that you had better do as you are bid. You will then begin to think what you are bid to do, and who bids it. And you will find, unless you are very unhappy indeed, that there is always a quite clear notion of right and wrong in your minds, which you can either obey or disobey, at your pleasure. Obey it simply and resolutely; it will become clearer to you every day: and in obedience to it, you will find a sense of being in harmony with nature, and at peace with God, and all His creatures. You will not understand how the peace comes, nor even in what it consists. It is the peace that passes understanding;—it is just as visionary and imaginative as love is, and just as real, and just as necessary to the life of man. It is the only source of true cheerfulness, and of true common sense; and whether you believe the Bible, or don't,—or believe the Koran, or don't—or believe the Vedas, or don't—it will enable you to believe in God, and please Him, and be such a part of the {Greek: *eudokia*} of the universe as your nature fits you to be, in His sight, faithful in awe to the powers that are above you, and gracious in regard to the creatures that are around.

225. I will take leave on this head to read one more piece of Carlyle, bearing much on present matters. "I hope also they will attack earnestly, and at length

extinguish and eradicate, this idle habit of 'accounting for the moral sense,' as they phrase it. A most singular problem;—instead of bending every thought to have more, and ever more, of 'moral sense,' and therewith to irradiate your own poor soul, and all its work, into something of divineness, as the one thing needful to you in this world! A very futile problem that other, my friends; futile, idle, and far worse; leading to what moral ruin, you little dream of! The moral sense, thank God, is a thing you never will 'account for;' that, if you could think of it, is the perennial miracle of man; in all times, visibly connecting poor transitory man, here on this bewildered earth, with his Maker who is eternal in the heavens. By no greatest happiness principle, greatest nobleness principle, or any principle whatever, will you make that in the least clearer than it already is;—forbear, I say, or you may darken it away from you altogether! 'Two things,' says the memorable Kant, deepest and most logical of metaphysical thinkers, 'two things strike me dumb: the infinite starry heavens; and the sense of right and wrong in man.' Visible infinites, both; say nothing of them; don't try to 'account for them;' for you can say nothing wise."

226. Very briefly, I must touch one or two further relative conditions in this natural history of the soul. I have asked you to take the metaphorical, but distinct, word '{Greek: *chrisma*}' rather than the direct but obscure one 'piety'; mainly because the Master of your religion chose the metaphorical epithet for the perpetual one of His own life and person.

But if you will spend a thoughtful hour or two in reading the scripture, which pious Greeks read, not indeed on daintily printed paper, but on daintily painted clay,—if you will examine, that is to say, the scriptures of the Athenian religion, on their Pan-Athenaic vases, in their faithful days, you will find that the gift of the literal {Greek: *chrisma*}, or anointing oil, to the victor in the kingly and visible contest of life, is signed always with the image of that spirit or goddess of the air who was the source of their invisible life. And let me, before quitting this part of my subject, give you one piece of what you will find useful counsel. If ever from the right apothecary, or {Greek: muropolaes}', you get any of that {Greek: *chrisma*},—don't be careful, when you set it by, of looking for dead dragons or dead dogs in it. But look out for the dead flies.

227. Again; remember, I only quote St. Paul as I quote Xenophon to you; but I expect you to get some good from both. As I want you to think what Xenophon means by '{Greek: *manteia*},' so I want you to consider also what St. Paul means by '{Greek: *prophetia*}.' He tells you to prove all things,—to hold fast what is good, and not to despise 'prophesyings.'

228. Now it is quite literally probable, that this world, having now for some five hundred years absolutely refused to do as it is plainly bid by every

prophet that ever spoke in any nation, and having reduced itself therefore to Saul's condition, when he was answered neither by Urim nor by prophets, may be now, while you sit there, receiving necromantic answers from the witch of Endor. But with that possibility you have no concern. There is a prophetic power in your own hearts, known to the Greeks, known to the Jews, known to the Apostles, and knowable by you. If it is now silent to you, do not despise it by tranquillity under that privation; if it speaks to you, do not despise it by disobedience.

229. Now in this broad definition of Pietas, as reverence to sentimental law, you will find I am supported by all classical authority and use of this word. For the particular meaning of which I am next about to use the word Religion, there is no such general authority, nor can there be, for any limited or accurate meaning of it. The best authors use the word in various senses; and you must interpret each writer by his own context. I have myself continually used the term vaguely. I shall endeavour, henceforward, to use it under limitations which, willing always to accept, I shall only transgress by carelessness, or compliance with some particular use of the word by others. The power in the word, then, which I wish you now to notice, is in its employment with respect to doctrinal divisions. You do not say that one man is of one piety, and another of another; but you do, that one man is of one religion, and another of another.

230. The religion of any man is thus properly to be interpreted, as the feeling which binds him, irrationally, to the fulfilment of duties, or acceptance of beliefs, peculiar to a certain company of which he forms a member, as distinct from the rest of the world. 'Which binds him *irrationally*,' I say;—by a feeling, at all events, apart from reason, and often superior to it; such as that which brings back the bee to its hive, and the bird to her nest.

A man's religion is the form of mental rest, or dwelling-place, which, partly, his fathers have gained or built for him, and partly, by due reverence to former custom, he has built for himself; consisting of whatever imperfect knowledge may have been granted, up to that time, in the land of his birth, of the Divine character, presence, and dealings; modified by the circumstances of surrounding life.

It may be, that sudden accession of new knowledge may compel him to cast his former idols to the moles and to the bats. But it must be some very miraculous interposition indeed which can justify him in quitting the religion of his forefathers; and, assuredly, it must be an unwise interposition which provokes him to insult it.

231. On the other hand, the value of religious ceremonial, and the virtue of religious truth, consist in the meek fulfilment of the one as the fond habit of a family; and the meek acceptance of the other, as the narrow knowledge of

a child. And both are destroyed at once, and the ceremonial or doctrinal prejudice becomes only an occasion of sin, if they make us either wise in our own conceit, or violent in our methods of proselytism. Of those who will compass sea and land to make one proselyte, it is too generally true that they are themselves the children of hell, and make their proselytes twofold more so.

232. And now I am able to state to you, in terms so accurately defined that you cannot misunderstand them, that we are about to study the results in Italy of the victory of an impious Christian over a pious Infidel, in a contest which, if indeed principalities of evil spirit are ever permitted to rule over the darkness of this world, was assuredly by them wholly provoked, and by them finally decided. The war was not actually ended until the battle of Tagliacozzo, fought in August, 1268; but you need not recollect that irregular date, or remember it only as three years after the great battle of Welcome, Benevento; which was the decisive one. Recollect, therefore, securely:

1250. The First Trades Revolt in Florence.

1260. Battle of the Arbia.

1265. Battle of Welcome.

Then between the battle of Welcome and of Tagliacozzo, (which you might almost English in the real meaning of it as the battle of Hart's Death: 'cozzo' is a butt or thrust with the horn, and you may well think of the young Conradin as a wild hart or stag of the hills)—between those two battles, in 1266, comes the second and central revolt of the trades in Florence, of which I have to speak in next lecture.

233. The two German princes who perished in these two battles—Manfred of Tarentum, and his nephew and ward Conradin—are the natural son, and the legitimate grandson of Frederick II.: they are also the last assertors of the infidel German power in south Italy against the Church; and in alliance with the Saracens; such alliance having been maintained faithfully ever since Frederick II.'s triumphal entry into Jerusalem, and cornation as its king. Not only a great number of Manfred's forts were commanded by Saracen governors, but he had them also appointed over civil tribunals. My own impression is that he found the Saracens more just and trustworthy than the Christians; but it is proper to remember the allegations of the Church against the whole Suabian family; namely, that Manfred had smothered his father Frederick under cushions at Ferentino; and that, of Frederick's sons, Conrad had poisoned Henry, and Manfred had poisoned Conrad. You will, however, I believe, find the Prince Manfred one of the purest representatives of northern chivalry. Against his nephew, educated in all knightly accomplishment by his mother, Elizabeth of Bavaria, nothing could be

alleged by his enemies, even when resolved on his death, but the splendour of his spirit and the brightness of his youth.

234. Of the character of their enemy, Charles of Anjou, there will remain on your minds, after careful examination of his conduct, only the doubt whether I am justified in speaking of him as Christian against Infidel. But you will cease to doubt this when you have entirely entered into the conditions of this nascent Christianity of the thirteenth century. You will find that while men who desire to be virtuous receive it as the mother of virtues, men who desire to be criminal receive it as the forgiver of crimes; and that therefore, between Ghibelline or Infidel cruelty, and Guelph or Christian cruelty, there is always this difference,—that the Infidel cruelty is done in hot blood, and the Christian's in cold. I hope (in future lectures on the architecture of Pisa) to illustrate to you the opposition between the Ghibelline Conti, counts, and the Guelphic Visconti, viscounts or "against counts," which issues, for one thing, in that, by all men blamed as too deliberate, death of the Count Ugolino della Gherardesca. The Count Ugolino was a traitor, who entirely deserved death; but another Count of Pisa, entirely faithful to the Ghibelline cause, was put to death by Charles of Anjou, not only in cold blood, but with resolute infliction of Ugolino's utmost grief;—not in the dungeon, but in the full light of day—his son being first put to death before his eyes. And among the pieces of heraldry most significant in the middle ages, the asp on the shield of the Guelphic viscounts is to be much remembered by you as a sign of this merciless cruelty of mistaken religion; mistaken, but not in the least hypocritical. It has perfect confidence in itself, and can answer with serenity for all its deeds. The serenity of heart never appears in the guilty Infidels; they die in despair or gloom, greatly satisfactory to adverse religious minds.

235. The French Pope, then, Urban of Troyes, had sent for Charles of Anjou; who would not have answered his call, even with all the strength of Anjou and Provence, had not Scylla of the Tyrrhene Sea been on his side. Pisa, with eighty galleys (the Sicilian fleet added to her own), watched and defended the coasts of Rome. An irresistible storm drove her fleet to shelter; and Charles, in a single ship, reached the mouth of the Tiber, and found lodgings at Rome in the convent of St. Paul. His wife meanwhile spent her dowry in increasing his land army, and led it across the Alps. How he had got his wife, and her dowry, we must hear in Villani's words, as nearly as I can give their force in English, only, instead of the English word pilgrim, I shall use the Italian 'romeo' for the sake both of all English Juliets, and that you may better understand the close of the sixth canto of the Paradise.

236. "Now the Count Raymond Berenger had for his inheritance all Provence on this side Rhone; and he was a wise and courteous signor, and of noble state, and virtuous; and in his time they did honourable things; and to his court came by custom all the gentlemen of Provence, and France, and

Catalonia, for his courtesy and noble state; and there they made many cobbled verses, and Provençal songs of great sentences."

237. I must stop to tell you that 'cobbled' or 'coupled' verses mean rhymes, as opposed to the dull method of Latin verse; for we have now got an ear for jingle, and know that dove rhymes to love. Also, "songs of great sentences" mean didactic songs, containing much in little, (like the new didactic Christian painting,) of which an example (though of a later time) will give you a better idea than any description.

"Vraye foy de necessité,

Non tant seulement d'equité,

Nous fait de Dieu sept choses croire:

C'est sa doulce nativité,

Son baptesme d'humilité,

Et sa mort, digne de mémoire:

Son descens en la chartre noire,

Et sa resurrection, voire;

S'ascencion d'auctorité,

La venue judicatoire,

Ou ly bons seront mis en gloire,

Et ly mals en adversité."

238. "And while they were making these cobbled verses and harmonious creeds, there came a romeo to court, returning from the shrine of St. James." I must stop again just to say that he ought to have been called a pellegrino, not a romeo, for the three kinds of wanderers are,—Palmer, one who goes to the Holy Land; Pilgrim, one who goes to Spain; and Romeo, one who goes to Rome. Probably this romeo had been to both. "He stopped at Count Raymond's court, and was so wise and worthy (valoroso), and so won the Count's grace, that he made him his master and guide in all things. Who also, maintaining himself in honest and religious customs of life, in a little time, by his industry and good sense, doubled the Count's revenues three times over, maintaining always a great and honoured court. Now the Count had four daughters, and no son; and by the sense and provision of the good romeo— (I can do no better than translate 'procaccio' provision, but it is only a makeshift for the word derived from procax, meaning the general talent of prudent impudence, in getting forward; 'forwardness,' has a good deal of the true sense, only diluted;)—well, by the sense and—progressive faculty, shall

we say?—of the good pilgrim, he first married the eldest daughter, by means of money, to the good King Louis of France, saying to the Count, 'Let me alone,—Lascia-mi-fare—and never mind the expense, for if you marry the first one well, I'll marry you all the others cheaper, for her relationship."

239. "And so it fell out, sure enough; for incontinently the King of England (Henry III.) because he was the King of France's relation, took the next daughter, Eleanor, for very little money indeed; next, his natural brother, elect King of the Romans, took the third; and, the youngest still remaining unmarried,—says the good romeo, 'Now for this one, I will you to have a strong man for son-in-law, who shall be thy heir;'—and so he brought it to pass. For finding Charles, Count of Anjou, brother of the King Louis, he said to Raymond, "'Give her now to him, for his fate is to be the best man in the world,'—prophesying of him. And so it was done. And after all this it came to pass, by envy which ruins all good, that the barons of Provence became jealous of the good romeo, and accused him to the Count of having ill-guided his goods, and made Raymond demand account of them. Then the good romeo said, 'Count, I have served thee long, and have put thee from little state into mighty, and for this, by false counsel of thy people, thou art little grateful. I came into thy court a poor romeo; I have lived honestly on thy means; now, make to be given to me my little mule and my staff and my wallet, as I came, and I will make thee quit of all my service.' The Count would not he should go; but for nothing would he stay; and so he came, and so he departed, that no one ever knew whence he had come, nor whither he went. It was the thought of many that he was indeed a sacred spirit."

240. This pilgrim, you are to notice, is put by Dante in the orb of justice, as a just servant; the Emperor Justinian being the image of a just ruler. Justinian's law-making turned out well for England; but the good romeo's match-making ended ill for it; and for Borne, and Naples also. For Beatrice of Provence resolved to be a queen like her three sisters, and was the prompting spirit of Charles's expedition to Italy. She was crowned with him, Queen of Apulia and Sicily, on the day of the Epiphany, 1265; she and her husband bringing gifts that day of magical power enough; and Charles, as soon as the feast of coronation was over, set out to give battle to Manfred and his Saracens. "And this Charles," says Villani, "was wise, and of sane counsel; and of prowess in arms, and fierce, and much feared and redoubted by all the kings in the world;—magnanimous and of high purposes; fearless in the carrying forth of every great enterprise; firm in every adversity; a verifier of his every word; speaking little,—doing much; and scarcely ever laughed, and then but a little; sincere, and without flaw, as a religious and catholic person; stern in justice, and fierce in look; tall and nervous in person, olive coloured, and with a large nose, and well he appeared a royal majesty more than other men. Much he watched, and little he slept; and used to say

that so much time as one slept, one lost; generous to his men-at-arms, but covetous to acquire land, signory, and coin, come how it would, to furnish his enterprises and wars: in courtiers, servants of pleasure, or jocular persons, he delighted never."

241. To this newly crowned and resolute king, riding south from Rome, Manfred, from his vale of Nocera under Mount St. Augelo, sends to offer conditions of peace. Jehu the son of Nimshi is not swifter of answer to Ahaziah's messenger than the fiery Christian king, in his 'What hast thou to do with peace?' Charles answers the messengers with his own lips: "Tell the Sultan of Nocera, this day I will put him in hell, or he shall put me in paradise."

242. Do not think it the speech of a hypocrite. Charles was as fully prepared for death that day as ever Scotch Covenanter fighting for his Holy League; and as sure that death would find him, if it found, only to glorify and bless. Balfour of Burley against Claverhouse is not more convinced in heart that he draws the sword of the Lord and of Gideon. But all the knightly pride of Claverhouse himself is knit together, in Charles, with fearless faith, and religious wrath. "This Saracen scum, led by a bastard German,—traitor to his creed, usurper among his race,—dares it look me, a Christian knight, a prince of the house of France, in the eyes? Tell the Sultan of Nocera, to-day I put him in hell, or he puts me in paradise."

They are not passionate words neither; any more than hypocritical ones. They are measured, resolute, and the fewest possible. He never wasted words, nor showed his mind, but when he meant it should be known.

243. The messenger returned, thus answered; and the French king rode on with his host. Manfred met him in the plain of Grandella, before Benevento. I have translated the name of the fortress 'Welcome.' It was altered, as you may remember, from Maleventum, for better omen; perhaps, originally, only {Greek: *maloeis*}—a rock full of wild goats?—associating it thus with the meaning of Tagliacozzo.

244. Charles divided his army into four companies. The captain of his own was our English Guy de Montfort, on whom rested the power and the fate of his grandfather, the pursuer of the Waldensian shepherds among the rocks of the wild goats. The last, and it is said the goodliest, troop was of the exiled Guelphs of Florence, under Guido Guerra, whose name you already know. "These," said Manfred, as he watched them ride into their ranks, "cannot lose to-day." He meant that if he himself was the victor, he would restore these exiles to their city. The event of the battle was decided by the treachery of the Count of Caserta, Manfred's brother-in-law. At the end of the day only a few knights remained with him, whom he led in the last charge. As he helmed himself, the crest fell from his helmet. "Hoc est signum Dei," he said,—so

accepting what he saw to be the purpose of the Ruler of all things; not claiming God as his friend. not asking anything of Him, as if His purpose could be changed; not fearing Him as an enemy; but accepting simply His sign that the appointed day of death was come. He rode into the battle armed like a nameless soldier, and lay unknown among the dead.

245. And in him died all southern Italy. Never, after that day's treachery, did her nobles rise, or her people prosper.

Of the finding of the body of Manfred, and its casting forth, accursed, you may read, if you will, the story in Dante. I trace for you to-day rapidly only the acts of Charles after this victory, and its consummation, three years later, by the defeat of Conradin.

The town of Benevento had offered no resistance to Charles, but he gave it up to pillage, and massacred its inhabitants. The slaughter, indiscriminate, continued for eight days; the women and children were slain with the men, being of Saracen blood. Manfred's wife, Sybil of Epirus, his children, and all his barons, died, or were put to death, in the prisons of Provence. With the young Conrad, all the faithful Ghibel-line knights of Pisa were put to death. The son of Frederick of Antioch, who drove the Guelphs from Florence, had his eyes torn out, and was hanged, he being the last child of the house of Suabia. Twenty-four of the barons of Calabria were executed at Gallipoli, and at Home. Charles cut off the feet of those who had fought for Conrad; then—fearful lest they should be pitied—shut them into a house of wood, and burned them. His lieutenant in Sicily, William of the Standard, besieged the town of Augusta, which defended itself with some fortitude, but was betrayed, and all its inhabitants, (who must have been more than three thousand, for there were a thousand able to bear arms,) massacred in cold blood; the last of them searched for in their hiding-places, when the streets were empty, dragged to the sea-shore, then beheaded, and their bodies thrown into the sea. Throughout Calabria the Christian judges of Charles thus forgave his enemies. And the Mohammedan power and heresy ended in Italy, and she became secure in her Catholic creed.

246. Not altogether secure under French dominion. After fourteen years of misery, Sicily sang her angry vespers, and a Calabrian admiral burnt the fleet of Charles before his eyes, where Scylla rules her barking Salamis. But the French king died in prayerful peace, receiving the sacrament with these words of perfectly honest faith, as he reviewed his past life: "Lord God, as I truly believe that you are my Saviour, so I pray you to have mercy on my soul; and as I truly made the conquest of Sicily more to serve the Holy Church than for my own covetousness, so I pray you to pardon my sins."

247. You are to note the two clauses of this prayer. He prays absolute mercy, on account of his faith in Christ; but remission of purgatory, in proportion

to the quantity of good work he has done, or meant to do, as against evil. You are so much wiser in these days, you think, not believing in purgatory; and so much more benevolent,—not massacring women and children. But we must not be too proud of not believing in purgatory, unless we are quite sure of our real desire to be purified: and as to our not massacring children, it is true that an English gentleman will not now himself willingly put a knife into the throat either of a child or a lamb; but he will kill any quantity of children by disease in order to increase his rents, as unconcernedly as he will eat any quantity of mutton. And as to absolute massacre, I do not suppose a child feels so much pain in being killed as a full-grown man, and its life is of less value to it. No pain either of body or thought through which you could put an infant, would be comparable to that of a good son, or a faithful lover, dying slowly of a painful wound at a distance from a family dependent upon him, or a mistress devoted to him. But the victories of Charles, and the massacres, taken in sum, would not give a muster-roll of more than twenty thousand dead; men, women, and children counted all together. On the plains of France, since I first began to speak to you on the subject of the arts of peace, at least five hundred thousand men, in the prime of life, have been massacred by the folly of one Christian emperor, the insolence of another, and the mingling of mean rapacity with meaner vanity, which Christian nations now call 'patriotism.'

248. But that the Crusaders, (whether led by St. Louis or by his brother,) who habitually lived by robbery, and might be swiftly enraged to murder, were still too savage to conceive the spirit or the character of this Christ whose cross they wear, I have again and again alleged to you; not, I imagine, without question from many who have been accustomed to look to these earlier ages as authoritative in doctrine, if not in example. We alike err in supposing them more spiritual or more dark, than our own. They had not yet attained to the knowledge which we have despised, nor dispersed from their faith the shadows with which we have again overclouded ours.

Their passions, tumultuous and merciless as the Tyrrhene Sea, raged indeed with the danger, but also with the uses, of naturally appointed storm; while ours, pacific in corruption, languish in vague maremma of misguided pools; and are pestilential most surely as they retire.

LECTURE X.
FLEUR DE LYS.

249. Through all the tempestuous winter which during the period of

history we have been reviewing, weakened, in their war with the opposed

rocks of religious or knightly pride, the waves of the Tuscan Sea,

there has been slow increase of the Favonian power which is to bring

fruitfulness to the rock, peace to the wave. The new element which is

introduced in the thirteenth century, and perfects for a little time the

work of Christianity, at least in some few chosen souls, is the law of

Order and Charity, of intellectual and moral virtue, which it now became

the function of every great artist to teach, and of every true citizen

to maintain.

250. I have placed on your table one of the earliest existing engravings by a Florentine hand, representing the conception which the national mind formed of this spirit of order and tranquillity, "Cosmico," or the Equity of Kosmos, not by senseless attraction, but by spiritual thought and law. He stands pointing with his left hand to the earth, set only with tufts of grass; in his right hand he holds the ordered system of the universe—heaven and earth in one orb;—the heaven made cosmic by the courses of its stars; the earth cosmic by

{Illustration: PLATE IX.—THE CHARGE TO ADAM. MODERN ITALIAN. }

the seats of authority and fellowship,—castles on the hills and cities in the plain.

251. The tufts of grass under the feet of this figure will appear to you, at first, grotesquely formal. But they are only the simplest expression, in such herbage, of the subjection of all vegetative force to this law of order, equity, or symmetry, which, made by the Greek the principal method of his current vegetative sculpture, subdues it, in the hand of Cora or Triptolemus, into the merely triple sceptre, or animates it, in Florence, to the likeness of the Fleur-de-lys.

252. I have already stated to you that if any definite flower is meant by these triple groups of leaves, which take their authoritatively typical form in the crowns of the Cretan and Laciuian Hera, it is not the violet, but the purple iris; or sometimes, as in Pindar's description of the birth of Ismus, the yellow

water-flag, which you know so well in spring, by the banks of your Oxford streams. {1} But, in general, it means simply the springing of beautiful and orderly vegetation in fields upon which the dew falls pure. It is the expression, therefore, of peace on the redeemed and cultivated earth, and of the pleasure of heaven in the uncareful happiness of men clothed without labour, and fed without fear.

{Footnote 1: In the catalogues of the collection of drawings in this room, and in my "Queen of the Air" you will find all that I would ask you to notice about the various names and kinds of the flower, and their symbolic use.— Note only, with respect to our present purpose, that while the true white lily is placed in the hands of the Angel of the Annunciation even by Florentine artists, in their general design, the fleur-de-lys is given to him by Giovaiini Pisano on the façade of Orvieto; and that the flower in the crown-circlets of European kings answers, as I stated to you in my lecture on the Corona, to the Narcissus fillet of early Greece; the crown of abundance and rejoicing.}

253. In the passage, so often read by us, which announces the advent of Christianity as the dawn of peace on earth, we habitually neglect great part of the promise, owing to the false translation of the second clause of the sentence. I cannot understand how it should be still needful to point out to you here in Oxford that neither the Greek words {Greek: *"en anthriopois evdokia,"*} nor those of the vulgate, "in terra pax hominibus bonæ voluntatis," in the slightest degree justify our English words, "goodwill to men."

Of God's goodwill to men, and to all creatures, for ever, there needed no proclamation by angels. But that men should be able to please *Him*,—that their wills should be made holy, and they should not only possess peace in themselves, but be able to give joy to their God, in the sense in which He afterwards is pleased with His own baptized Son;—this was a new thing for Angels to declare, and for shepherds to believe.

254. And the error was made yet more fatal by its repetition in a passage of parallel importance,—the thanksgiving, namely, offered by Christ, that His Father, while He had hidden what it was best to know, not from the wise and prudent, but from some among the wise and prudent, and had revealed it unto babes; not 'for so it seemed good' in His sight, but 'that there might be well pleasing in His sight,'—namely, that the wise and simple might equally live in the necessary knowledge, and enjoyed presence, of God. And if, having accurately read these vital passages, you then as carefully consider the tenour of the two songs of human joy in the birth of Christ, the Magnificat, and the Nunc dimittis, you will find the theme of both to be, not the newness of blessing, but the equity which disappoints the cruelty and humbles the strength of men; which scatters the proud in the imagination of their hearts;

which fills the hungry with good things; and is not only the glory of Israel, but the light of the Gentiles.

255. As I have been writing these paragraphs, I have been checking myself almost at every word,—wondering, Will they be restless on their seats at this, and thinking all the while that they did not come here to be lectured on Divinity? You may have been a little impatient,—how could it well be otherwise? Had I been explaining points of anatomy, and showing you how you bent your necks and straightened your legs, you would have thought me quite in my proper function; because then, when you went with a party of connoisseurs through the Vatican, you could point out to them the insertion of the clavicle in the Apollo Belvidere; and in the Sistine Chapel the perfectly accurate delineation of the tibia in the legs of Christ. Doubtless; but you know I am lecturing at present on the goffi, and not on Michael Angelo; and the goffi are very careless about clavicles and shin-bones; so that if, after being lectured on anatomy, you went into the Campo Santo of Pisa, you would simply find nothing to look at, except three tolerably well-drawn skeletons. But if after being lectured on theology, you go into the Campo Santo of Pisa, you will find not a little to look at, and to remember.

256. For a single instance, you know Michael Angelo is admitted to have been so far indebted to these goffi as to borrow from the one to whose study of mortality I have just referred, Orcagna, the gesture of his Christ in the Judgment, He borrowed, however, accurately speaking, the position only, not the gesture; nor the meaning of it. {1} You all remember the action of Michael Angelo's Christ,—the right hand raised as if in violence of reprobation; and the left closed across His breast, as refusing all mercy. The action is one which appeals to persons of very ordinary sensations, and is very naturally adopted by the Renaissance painter, both for its popular effect, and its capabilities for the exhibition of his surgical science. But the old painter-theologian, though indeed he showed the right hand of Christ lifted, and the left hand laid across His breast, had another meaning in the actions. The fingers of the left hand are folded, in both the figures; but in Michael Angelo's as if putting aside an appeal; in Orcagna's, the fingers are bent to draw back the drapery from the right side. The right hand is raised by Michael Angelo as in anger; by Orcagna, only to show the wounded palm. And as, to the believing disciples, He showed them His hands and His side, so that they were glad,—so, to the unbelievers, at their judgment, He shows the wounds in hand and side. They shall look on Him whom they pierced.

{Footnote: I found all this in M. Didron's Iconographie, above quoted; I had never noticed the difference between the two figures myself.}

257. And thus, as we follow our proposed examination of the arts of the Christian centuries, our understanding of their work will be absolutely limited

by the degree of our sympathy with the religion which our fathers have bequeathed to us. You cannot interpret classic marbles without knowing and loving your Pindar and Æschylus, neither can you interpret Christian pictures without knowing and loving your Isaiah and Matthew. And I shall have continually to examine texts of the one as I would verses of the other; nor must you retract yourselves from the labour in suspicion that I desire to betray your scepticism, or undermine your positivism, because I recommend to you the accurate study of books which have hitherto been the light of the world.

258. The change, then, in the minds of their readers at this date, which rendered it possible for them to comprehend the full purport of Christianity, was in the rise of the new desire for equity and rest, amidst what had hitherto been mere lust for spoil, and joy in battle. The necessity for justice was felt in the now extending commerce; the desire of rest in the now pleasant and fitly furnished habitation; and the energy which formerly could only be satisfied in strife, now found enough both of provocation and antagonism in the invention of art, and the forces of nature. I have in this course of lectures endeavoured to fasten your attention on the Florentine Revolution of 1250, because its date is so easily memorable, and it involves the principles of every subsequent one, so as to lay at once the foundations of whatever greatness Florence afterwards achieved by her mercantile and civic power. But I must not close even this slight sketch of the central history of Val d'Aruo without requesting you, as you find time, to associate in your minds, with this first revolution, the effects of two which followed it, being indeed necessary parts of it, in the latter half of the century.

259. Remember then that the first, in 1250, is embryonic; and the significance of it is simply the establishment of order, and justice against violence and iniquity. It is equally against the power of knights and priests, so far as either are unjust,—not otherwise.

When Manfred fell at Benevento, his lieutenant, the Count Guido Novello, was in command of Florence. He was just, but weak; and endeavoured to temporize with the Guelphs. His effort ought to be notable to you, because it was one of the wisest and most far-sighted ever made in Italy; but it failed for want of resolution, as the gentlest and best men are too apt to fail. He brought from Bologna two knights of the order—then recently established— of joyful brethren; afterwards too fatally corrupted, but at this time pure in purpose. They constituted an order of chivalry which was to maintain peace, obey the Church, and succour widows and orphans; but to be bound by no monastic vows. Of these two knights, he chose one Guelph, the other Ghibelline; and under their balanced power Gruido hoped to rank the forces of the civil, manufacturing, and trading classes, divided into twelve corporations of higher and lower arts. {1} But the moment this beautiful arrangement was made, all parties—Guelph, Ghibelline, and popular,— turned unanimously against Count Guido Novello. The benevolent but irresolute captain indeed gathered his men into the square of the Trinity; but the people barricaded the streets issuing from it; and Guido, heartless, and unwilling for civil warfare, left the city with his Germans in good order. And so ended the incursion of the infidel Tedeschi for this time. The Florentines then dismissed the merry brothers whom the Tedeschi had set over them, and besought help from Orvieto and Charles of Anjou; who sent them Guy de Montfort and eight hundred French riders; the blessing of whose presence thus, at their own request, was granted them on Easter Day, 1267.

{Footnote: The seven higher arts were, Lawyers, Physicians, Bankers, Merchants of Foreign Goods, Wool Manufacturers, Silk Manufacturers, Furriers. The five lower arts were, Retail Sellers of Cloth, Butchers, Shoemakers, Masons and Carpenters, Smiths.}

On Candlemas, if you recollect, 1251, they open their gates to the Germans; and on Easter, 1267, to the French.

260. Remember, then, this revolution, as coming between the battles of Welcome and Tagliacozzo; and that it expresses the lower revolutionary temper of the trades, with English and French assistance. Its immediate result was the appointment of five hundred and sixty lawyers, woolcombers, and butchers, to deliberate upon all State questions,—under which happy ordinances you will do well, in your own reading, to leave Florence, that you may watch, for a while, darling little Pisa, all on fire for the young Conradin. She sent ten vessels across the Gulf of Genoa to fetch him; received his cavalry in her plain of Sarzana; and putting five thousand of her own best sailors into thirty ships, sent them to do what they could, all down the coast of Italy. Down they went; startling Gaeta with an attack as they passed; found Charles of Anjou's French and Sicilian fleet at Messina, fought it, beat it, and burned twenty-seven of its ships.

261. Meantime, the Florentines prospered as they might with their religious-democratic constitution,—until the death, in the odour of sanctity, of Charles of Anjou, and of that Pope Martin IV. whose tomb was destroyed with Urban's at Perugia. Martin died, as you may remember, of eating Bolsena eels,—that being his share in the miracles of the lake; and you will do well to remember at the same time, that the price of the lake eels was three soldi a pound; and that Niccola of Pisa worked at Siena for six soldi a day, and his son Giovanni for four.

262. And as I must in this place bid farewell, for a time, to Niccola and to his son, let me remind you of the large commission which the former received on the occasion of the battle of Tagliacozzo, and its subsequent massacres, when the victor, Charles, having to his own satisfaction exterminated the

seed of infidelity, resolves, both in thanksgiving, and for the sake of the souls of the slain knights for whom some hope might yet be religiously entertained, to found an abbey on the battle-field. In which purpose he sent for Niccola to Naples, and made him build on the field of Tagliacozzo, a church and abbey of the richest; and caused to be buried therein the infinite number of the bodies of those who died in that battle day; ordering farther, that, by many monks, prayer should be made for their souls, night and day. In which fabric the king was so pleased with Niccola's work that he rewarded and honoured him highly.

263. Do you not begin to wonder a little more what manner of man this Nicholas was, who so obediently throws down the towers which offend the Ghibelliues, and so skilfully puts up the pinnacles which please the Guelphs? A passive power, seemingly, he;—plastic in the hands of any one who will employ him to build, or to throw down. On what exists of evidence, demonstrably in these years here is the strongest brain of Italy, thus for six shilling a day doing what it is bid.

264. I take farewell of him then, for a little time, ratifying to you, as far as my knowledge permits, the words of my first master in Italian art, Lord Lindsay.

"In comparing the advent of Niccola Pisano to that of the sun at his rising, I am conscious of no exaggeration; on the contrary, it is the only simile by which I can hope to give you an adequate impression of his brilliancy and power relatively to the age in which he flourished. Those sons of Erebus, the American Indians, fresh from their traditional subterranean world, and gazing for the first time on the gradual dawning of the day in the East, could not have been more dazzled, more astounded, when the sun actually appeared, than the popes and podestas, friars and freemasons must have been in the thirteenth century, when from among the Biduinos, Bonannos, and Antealmis of the twelfth, Niccola emerged in his glory, sovereign and supreme, a fount of light, diffusing warmth and radiance over Christendom. It might be too much to parallel him in actual genius with Dante and Shakspeare; they stand alone and unapproachable, each on his distinct pinnacle of the temple of Christian song; and yet neither of them can boast such extent and durability of influence, for whatever of highest excellence has been achieved in sculpture and painting, not in Italy only, but throughout Europe, has been in obedience to the impulse he primarily gave, and in following up the principle which he first struck out.

"His latter days were spent in repose at Pisa, but the precise year of his death is uncertain; Vasari fixes it in 1275; it could not have been much later. He was buried in the Campo Santo. Of his personal character we, alas! know nothing; even Shakspeare is less a stranger to us. But that it was noble, simple, and consistent, and free from the petty foibles that too frequently beset genius, may be fairly presumed from the works he has left behind him, and from the eloquent silence of tradition."

265. Of the circumstances of Niccola Pisano's death, or the ceremonials practised at it, we are thus left in ignorance.

The more exemplary death of Charles of Aujou took place on the 7th of January, then, 1285; leaving the throne of Naples to a boy of twelve; and that of Sicily, to a Prince of Spain. Various discord, between French, Spanish, and Calabrese vices, thenceforward paralyzes South Italy, and Florence becomes the leading power of the Guelph faction. She had been inflamed and pacified through continual paroxysms of civil quarrel during the decline of Charles's power; but, throughout, the influence of the nobles declines, by reason of their own folly and insolence; while the people, though with no small degree of folly and insolence on their own side, keep hold of their main idea of justice. In the meantime, similar assertions of law against violence, and the nobility of useful occupation, as compared with that of idle rapine, take place in Bologna, Siena, and even at Rome, where Bologna sends her senator, Branca Leone, (short for Branca-di-Leone, Lion's Grip,) whose inflexible and rightly guarded reign of terror to all evil and thievish persons, noble or other, is one of the few passages of history during the middle ages, in which the real power of civic virtue may be seen exercised without warping by party spirit, or weakness of vanity or fear.

266. And at last, led by a noble, Giano della Bella, the people of Florence write and establish their final condemnation of noblesse living by rapine, those 'Ordinamenti della Giustizia,' which practically excluded all idle persons from government, and determined that the priors, or leaders of the State, should be priors, or leaders of its arts and productive labour; that its head 'podesta' or 'power' should be the standard-bearer of justice; and its council or parliament composed of charitable men, or good men: "boni viri," in the sense from which the French formed their noun 'bonte.'

The entire governing body was thus composed, first, of the Podestas, standard-bearer of justice; then of his military captain; then of his lictor, or executor; then of the twelve priors of arts and liberties—properly, deliberators on the daily occupations, interests, and pleasures of the body politic;—and, finally, of the parliament of "kind men," whose business was to determine what kindness could be shown to other states, by way of foreign policy.

267. So perfect a type of national government has only once been reached in the history of the human race. And in spite of the seeds of evil in its own impatience, and in the gradually increasing worldliness of the mercantile body; in spite of the hostility of the angry soldier, and the malignity of the sensual priest, this government gave to Europe the entire cycle of Christian

art, properly so called, and every highest Master of labour, architectural, scriptural, or pictorial, practised in true understanding of the faith of Christ;—Orcagna, Giotto, Brunelleschi, Lionardo, Luini as his pupil, Lippi, Luca, Angelico, Botticelli, and Michael Angelo.

268. I have named two men, in this group, whose names are more familiar to your ears than any others, Angelico and Michael Angelo;—who yet are absent from my list of those whose works I wish you to study, being both extravagant in their enthusiasm,—the one for the nobleness of the spirit, and the other for that of the flesh. I name them now, because the gifts each had were exclusively Florentine; in whatever they have become to the mind of Europe since, they are utterly children of the Val d'Arno.

269. You are accustomed, too carelessly, to think of Angelico as a child of the Church, rather than of Florence. He was born in 1387,—just eleven years, that is to say, after the revolt of Florence *against* the Church, and ten after the endeavour of the Church to recover her power by the massacres of Faenza and Cesena. A French and English army of pillaging riders were on the other side of the Alps,—six thousand strong; the Pope sent for it; Robert Cardinal of Geneva brought it into Italy. The Florentines fortified their Apennines against it; but it took winter quarters at Cesena, where the Cardinal of Geneva massacred five thousand persons in a day, and the children and sucklings were literally dashed against the stones.

270. That was the school which the Christian Church had prepared for their brother Angelica. But Fèsole, secluding him in the shade of her mount of Olives, and Florence revealing to him the true voice of his Master, in the temple of St. Mary of the Flower, taught him his lesson of peace on earth, and permitted him his visions of rapture in heaven. And when the massacre of Cesena was found to have been in vain, and the Church was compelled to treat with the revolted cities who had united to mourn for her victories, Florence sent her a living saint, Catherine of Siena, for her political Ambassador.

271. Of Michael Angelo I need not tell you: of the others, we will read the lives, and think over them one by one; the great fact which I have written this course of lectures to enforce upon your minds is the dependence of all the arts on the virtue of the State, and its kindly order.

The absolute mind and state of Florence, for the seventy years of her glory, from 1280 to 1350, you find quite simply and literally described in the 112th Psalm, of which I read you the descriptive verses, in the words in which they sang it, from this typically perfect manuscript of the time:—

Gloria et divitie in domo ejus, justitia ejus manet in seculum seculi.

Exortum est in tenebris lumen reotis, misericors, et miserator, et

Justus. Jocundus homo, qui miseretur, et commodat: disponet sermones suos in

judicio. Dispersit, dedit pauperibus; justitia ejus manet in seculum seculi;

cornu ejus exaltabitur in gloria.

I translate simply, praying you to note as the true one, the *literal* meaning of every word:—

Glory and riches are in his house. His justice remains for ever.

Light is risen in darkness for the straightforward people.

He is merciful in heart, merciful in deed, and just.

A jocund man; who is merciful, and lends.

He will dispose his words in judgment.

He hath dispersed. He hath given to the poor. His justice remain!

for ever. His horn shall be exalted in glory.

272. With vacillating, but steadily prevailing effort, the Florentines maintained this life and character for full half a century.

You will please now look at my staff of the year 1300, {Footnote: Page 33 in my second lecture on Engraving.} adding the names of Dante and Orcagna, having each their separate masterful or prophetic function.

That is Florence's contribution to the intellectual work of the world during these years of justice. Now, the promise of Christianity is given with lesson from the fleur-de-lys: Seek ye first the royalty of God, and His justice, "and all these things," material wealth, "shall be added unto you." It is a perfectly clear, perfectly literal,—never failing and never unfulfilled promise. There is no instance in the whole cycle of history of its not being accomplished,— fulfilled to the uttermost, with full measure, pressed down, and running over.

273. Now hear what Florence was, and what wealth she had got by her justice. In the year 1330, before she fell, she had within her walls a hundred and fifty thousand inhabitants, of whom all the men—(laity)—between the ages of fifteen and seventy, were ready at an instant to go out to war, under their banners, in number twenty-four thousand. The army of her entire territory was eighty thousand; and within it she counted fifteen hundred noble, families, every one absolutely submissive to her gonfalier of justice. She had within her walls a hundred and ten churches, seven priories, and thirty hospitals for the sick and poor; of foreign guests, on the average, fifteen hundred, constantly. From eight to ten thousand children were taught to read in her schools. The town was surrounded by some fifty square miles of uninterrupted garden, of olive, corn, vine, lily, and rose.

And the monetary existence of England and France depended upon her wealth. Two of her bankers alone had lent Edward III. of England five millions of money (in sterling value of this present hour).

274. On the 10th of March, 1337, she was first accused, with truth, of selfish breach of treaties. On the 10th of April, all her merchants in France were imprisoned by Philip Valois; and presently afterwards Edward of England failed, quite in your modern style, for his five millions. These money losses would have been nothing to her; but on the 7th of August, the captain of her army, Pietro de' Rossi of Parma, the unquestioned best knight in Italy, received a chance spear-stroke before Monselice, and died next day. He was the Bayard of Italy; and greater than Bayard, because living in a nobler time. He never had failed in any military enterprise, nor ever stained success with cruelty or shame. Even the German troops under him loved him without bounds. To his companions he gave gifts with such largesse, that his horse and armour were all that at any time he called his own. Beautiful and pure as Sir Galahad, all that was brightest in womanhood watched and honoured him.

And thus, 8th August, 1337, he went to his own place.—To-day I trace the fall of Florence no more.

I will review the points I wish you to remember; and briefly meet, so far as I can, the questions which I think should occur to you.

275. I have named Edward III. as our heroic type of Franchise. And yet I have but a minute ago spoken of him as 'failing' in quite your modern manner. I must correct my expression:—he had no intent of failing when he borrowed; and did not spend his money on himself. Nevertheless, I gave him as an example of frankness; but by no means of honesty. He is simply the boldest and royalest of Free Riders; the campaign of Crecy is, throughout, a mere pillaging foray. And the first point I wish you to notice is the difference in the pecuniary results of living by robbery, like Edward III., or by agriculture and just commerce, like the town of Florence. That Florence can lend five millions to the King of England, and loose them with little care, is the result of her olive gardens and her honesty. Now hear the financial phenomena attending military exploits, and a life of pillage.

276. I give you them in this precise year, 1338, in which the King of England failed to the Florentines.

"He obtained from the prelates, barons, and knights of the

{Illustration: PLATE X.—THE NATIVITY. GIOVANNI PISANO. }

shires, one half of their wool for this year—a very valuable and extraordinary grant. He seized all the tin "(above-ground, you mean Mr. Henry!)" in

Cornwall and Devonshire, took possession of the lands of all priories alien, and of the money, jewels, and valuable effects of the Lombard merchants. He demanded certain quantities of bread, corn, oats, and bacon, from each county; borrowed their silver plate from many abbeys, as well as great sums of money both abroad and at home; and pawned his crown for fifty thousand florins." {1}

{Footnote 1: Henry's "History of England," book iv., chap. i.}

He pawns his queen's jewels next year; and finally summons all the gentlemen of England who had forty pounds a year, to come and receive the honour of knighthood, or pay to be excused!

277. II. The failures of Edward, or of twenty Edwards, would have done Florence no harm, had she remained true to herself, and to her neighbouring states. Her merchants only fall by their own increasing avarice; and above all by the mercantile form of pillage, usury. The idea that money could beget money, though more absurd than alchemy, had yet an apparently practical and irresistibly tempting confirmation in the wealth of villains, and the success of fools. Alchemy, in its day, led to pure chemistry; and calmly yielded to the science it had fostered. But all wholesome indignation against usurers was prevented, in the Christian mind, by wicked and cruel religious hatred of the race of Christ. In the end, Shakspeare himself, in his fierce effort against the madness, suffered himself to miss his mark by making his usurer a Jew: the Franciscan institution of the Mount of Pity failed before the lust of Lombardy, and the logic of Augsburg; and, to this day, the worship of the Immaculate Virginity of Money, mother of the Omnipotence of Money, is the Protestant form of Madonna worship.

278. III. The usurer's fang, and the debtor's shame, might both have been trodden down under the feet of Italy, had her knights and her workmen remained true to each other. But the brotherhoods of Italy were not of Cain to Abel—but of Cain to Cain. Every man's sword was against his fellow. Pisa sank before Genoa at Meloria, the Italian Ægos-Potamos; Genoa before Venice in the war of Chiozza, the Italian siege of Syracuse. Florence sent her Brunelleschi to divert the waves of Serchio against the walls of Lucca; Lucca her Castruccio, to hold mock tournaments before the gates of vanquished Florence. The weak modern Italian reviles or bewails the acts of foreign races, as if his destiny had depended upon these; let him at least assume the pride, and bear the grief, of remembering that, among all the virgin cities of his country, there has not been one which would not ally herself with a stranger, to effect a sister's ruin.

279. Lastly. The impartiality with which I have stated the acts, so far as known to me, and impulses, so far as discernible by me, of the contending Church and Empire, cannot but give offence, or provoke suspicion, in the minds of

those among you who are accustomed to hear the cause of Religion supported by eager disciples, or attacked by confessed enemies. My confession of hostility would be open, if I were an enemy indeed; but I have never possessed the knowledge, and have long ago been cured of the pride, which makes men fervent in witness for the Church's virtue, or insolent in declamation against her errors. The will of Heaven, which grants the grace and ordains the diversities of Religion, needs no defence, and sustains no defeat, by the humours of men; and our first business in relation to it is to silence our wishes, and to calm our fears. If, in such modest and disciplined temper, you arrange your increasing knowledge of the history of mankind, you will have no final difficulty in distinguishing the operation of the Master's law from the consequences of the disobedience to it which He permits; nor will you respect the law less, because, accepting only the obedience of love, it neither hastily punishes, nor pompously rewards, with what men think reward or chastisement. Not always under the feet of Korah the earth is rent; not always at the call of Elijah the clouds gather; but the guarding mountains for ever stand round about Jerusalem; and the rain, miraculous evermore, makes green the fields for the evil and the good.

280. And if you will fix your minds only on the conditions of human life which the Giver of it demands, "He hath shown thee, oh man, what is good, and what doth thy Lord require of thee, but to do justice, and to love mercy, and to walk humbly with thy God," you will find that such obedience is always acknowledged by temporal blessing. If, turning from the manifest miseries of cruel ambition, and manifest wanderings of insolent belief, you summon to your thoughts rather the state of unrecorded multitudes, who laboured in silence, and adored in humility, widely as the snows of Christendom brought memory of the Birth of Christ, or her spring sunshine, of His Resurrection, you may know that the promise of the Bethlehem angels has been literally fulfilled; and will pray that your English fields, joyfully as the banks of Arno, may still dedicate their pure lilies to St. Mary of the Flower.

APPENDIX.
(NOTES ON THE PLATES ILLUSTRATING THIS VOLUME.)

In the delivery of the preceding Lectures, some account was given of the theologic design of the sculptures by Giovanni Pisano at Orvieto, which I intended to have printed separately, and in more complete form, in this Appendix. But my strength does not now admit of my fulfilling the half of my intentions, and I find myself, at present, tired, and so dead in feeling, that I have no quickness in interpretation, or skill in description of emotional work. I must content myself, therefore, for the time, with a short statement of the points which I wish the reader to observe in the Plates, and which were left unnoticed in the text.

The frontispiece is the best copy I can get, in permanent materials, of a photograph of the course of the Arno, through Pisa, before the old banks were destroyed. Two arches of the Ponte-a-Mare which was carried away in the inundation of 1870, are seen in the distance; the church of La Spina, in its original position overhanging the river; and the buttressed and rugged walls of the mediaeval shore. Never more, any of these, to be seen in reality, by living eyes.

PLATE I.—A small portion of a photograph of Nicolo Pisano's Adoration of the Magi, on the pulpit of the Pisan Baptistery. The intensely Greek character of the heads, and the severely impetuous chiselling (learned from Late Roman rapid work), which drives the lines of the drapery nearly straight, may be seen better in a fragment of this limited measure than in the crowded massing of the entire subject. But it may be observed also that there is both a thoughtfulness and a tenderness in the features, whether of the Virgin or the attendant angel, which already indicate an aim beyond that of Greek art.

PLATE II—The Pulpit of the Baptistery (of which the preceding plate represents a portion). I have only given this general view for convenience of reference. Beautiful photographs of the subject on a large scale are easily attainable.

PLATE III.—The Fountain of Perugia. Executed from a sketch by Mr. Arthur Severn. The perspective of the steps is not quite true; we both tried to get it right, but found that it would be a day or two's work, to little purpose, and so let them go at hazard. The inlaid pattern behind is part of the older wall of the cathedral; the late door is of course inserted.

PLATE IV., LETTER E.—From Norman Bible in the British Museum; showing the moral temper which regulated common ornamentation in the twelfth century.

PLATE V.—Door of the Baptistery at Pisa. The reader must note that, although these plates are necessarily, in fineness of detail, inferior to the photographs from which they are taken, they have the inestimable advantage of permanence, and will not fade away into spectres when the book is old. I am greatly puzzled by the richness of the current ornamentation on the main pillars, as opposed to the general severity of design. I never can understand how the men who indulged in this flowing luxury of foliage were so stern in their masonry and figure-draperies.

PLATE VI.—Part of the lintel of the door represented on Plate V., enlarged. I intended, in the Lecture on Marble Couchant, to have insisted, at some length, on the decoration of the lintel and side-posts, as one of the most important phases of mystic ecclesiastical sculpture. But I find the materials furnished by Lucca, Pisa, and Florence, for such an essay are far too rich to be examined cursorily; the treatment even of this single lintel could scarcely be enough explained in the close of the Lecture. I must dwell on some points of it now.

Look back to Section 175 in "Aratra Pentelici," giving statement of the four kinds of relief in sculpture. The uppermost of these plinths is of the kind I have called 'round relief'; you might strike it out on a coin. The lower is 'foliate relief'; it looks almost as if the figures had been cut out of one layer of marble, and laid against another behind it.

The uppermost, at the distance of my diagram, or in nature itself, would scarcely be distinguished at a careless glance from an egg-and-arrow moulding. You could not have a more simple or forcible illustration of my statement in the first chapter of "Aratra," that the essential business of sculpture is to produce a series of agreeable bosses or rounded surfaces; to which, if possible, some meaning may afterwards be attached. In the present instance, every egg becomes an angel, or evangelist, and every arrow a lily, or a wing. {1} The whole is in the most exquisitely finished Byzantine style.

{Footnote: In the contemporary south door of the Duomo of Genoa, the Greek moulding is used without any such transformation.}

I am not sure of being right in my interpretation of the meaning of these figures; but I think there can be little question about it. There are eleven altogether; the three central, Christ with His mother and St. Joseph; then, two evangelists, with two alternate angels, on each side. Each of these angels carries a rod, with a fleur-de-lys termination; their wings decorate the intermediate ridges (formed, in a pure Greek moulding, by the arrows); and, behind the heads of all the figures, there is now a circular recess; once filled, I doubt not, by a plate of gold. The Christ, and the Evangelists, all carry books, of which each has a mosaic, or intaglio ornament, in the shape of a cross. I could not show you a more severe or perfectly representative piece of *architectural* sculpture.

The heads of the eleven figures are as simply decorative as the ball flowers are in our English Gothic tracery; the slight irregularity produced by different gesture and character giving precisely the sort of change which a good designer wishes to see in the parts of a consecutive ornament.

The moulding closes at each extremity with a palm-tree, correspondent in execution with those on coins of Syracuse; for the rest, the interest of it consists only in these slight variations of attitude by which the figures express wonder or concern at some event going on in their presence. They are looking down; and I do not doubt, are intended to be the heavenly witnesses of the story engraved on the stone below,—The Life and Death of the Baptist.

The lower stone on which this is related, is a model of skill in Fiction, properly so called. In Fictile art, in Fictile history, it is equally exemplary. 'Feigning' or 'affecting' in the most exquisite way by fastening intensely on the principal points.

Ask yourselves what are the principal points to be insisted on, in the story of the Baptist.

He came, "preaching the Baptism of Repentance for the remission of sins." That is his Advice, or Order-preaching.

And he came, "to bear witness of the Light." "Behold the Lamb of God, which taketh away the sins of the world." That is his declaration, or revelation-preaching.

And the end of his own life is in the practice of this preaching—if you will think of it—under curious difficulties in both kinds. Difficulties in putting away sin—difficulties in obtaining sight. The first half of the stone begins with the apocalyptic preaching. Christ, represented as in youth, is set under two trees, in the wilderness. St. John is scarcely at first seen; he is only the guide, scarcely the teacher, of the crowd of peoples, nations, and languages, whom he leads, pointing them to the Christ. Without doubt, all these figures have separate meaning. I am too ignorant to interpret it; but observe generally, they are the thoughtful and wise of the earth, not its ruffians or rogues. This is not, by any means, a general amnesty to blackguards, and an apocalypse to brutes, which St. John is preaching. These are quite the best people he can find to call, or advise. You see many of them carry rolls of paper in their hands, as he does himself. In comparison with the books of the upper cornice, these have special meaning, as throughout Byzantine design.

"Adverte quod patriarchæ et prophetse pinguntur cum rotulis

in manibus; quidam vero apostoli cum libris, et quidam

cum rotulis. Nempe quia ante Christi adventum fides figurative

ostendebatur, et quoad multa, in se implicita erat. Ad

quod ostendendum patriarchse et prophetæ pinguntur cum rotulis,

per quos quasi qusedam imperfecta cognitio design atur;

quia vero apostoli a Christo perfecte edocti suut, ideo libris,

per quos designatur perfecta cognitio, uti possunt."

WILLIAM DURANDUS, *quoted by Didron, p. 305.*

PLATE VII.—Next to this subject of the preaching comes the Baptism: and then, the circumstances of St. John's death. First, his declaration to Herod, "It is not lawful for thee to have thy brother's wife:" on which he is seized and carried to prison:—next, Herod's feast,—the consultation between daughter and mother, "What shall I ask?"—the martyrdom, and burial by the disciples. The notable point in the treatment of all these subjects is the quiet and mystic Byzantine dwelling on thought rather than action. In a northern sculpture of this subject, the daughter of Herodias would have been assuredly dancing; and most probably, casting a somersault. With the Byzantine, the debate in her mind is the only subject of interest, and he carves above, the evil angels, laying their hands on the heads, first of Herod and Herodias, and then of Herodias and her daughter.

PLATE VIII.—The issuing of commandment not to eat of the tree of knowledge. (Orvieto Cathedral.)

This, with Plates X. and XII., will give a sufficiently clear conception to any reader who has a knowledge of sculpture, of the principles of Giovanni Pisano's design. I have thought it well worth while to publish opposite two of them, facsimiles of the engravings which profess to represent them in Gruiier's monograph {1} of the Orvieto sculptures; for these outlines will, once for all, and better than any words, show my pupils what is the real virue of mediaeval work,—the power which we medievalists rejoice in it for. Precisely the qualities which are *not* in the modern drawings, are the essential virtues of the early sculpture. If you like the Gruner outlines best, you need not trouble yourself to go to Orvieto, or anywhere else in Italy. Sculpture, such as those outlines represent, can be supplied to you by the acre, to order, in any modern academician's atelier. But if you like the strange, rude, quaint, Gothic realities (for these photographs are, up to a certain point, a vision of the reality) best; then, don't study mediaeval art under the direction of modern illustrators. Look at it—for however short a time, where you can find it—veritable and untouched, however mouldered or shattered. And abhor, as you would the mimicry of your best friend's manners by a fool, all restorations and improving copies. For remember, none but fools think they can restore—none, but worse fools, that they can improve.

{Footnote: The drawings are by some Italian draughtsman, whose name it is no business of mine to notice.}

Examine these outlines, then, with extreme care, and point by point. The things which they have refused or lost, are the things you have to love, in Giovanni Pisano.

I will merely begin the task of examination, to show you how to set about it. Take the head of the commanding Christ. Although inclined forward from the shoulders in the advancing motion of the whole body, the head itself is not stooped; but held entirely upright, the line of forehead sloping backwards. The command is given in calm authority; not in mean anxiety. But this was not expressive enough for the copyist,—"How much better *I* can show what is meant!" thinks he. So he puts the line of forehead and nose upright; projects the brow out of its straight line; and the expression then becomes,—"Now, be very careful, and mind what I say." Perhaps you like this 'improved' action better? Be it so; only, it is not Giovanni Pisano's design; but the modern Italian's.

Next, take the head of Eve. It is much missed in the photograph—nearly all the finest lines lost—but enough is got to show Giovanni's mind.

It appears, he liked long-headed people, with sharp chins and straight noses. It might be very wrong of him; but that was his taste. So much so, indeed, that Adam and Eve have,

{Illustration: PLATE XI.—THE NATIVITY. MODERN ITALIAN.}

both of them, heads not much shorter than one-sixth of their entire height.

Your modern Academy pupil, of course, cannot tolerate this monstrosity. He indulgently corrects Giovanni, and Adam and Eve have entirely orthodox one-eighth heads, by rule of schools.

But how of Eve's sharp-cut nose and pointed chin, thin lips, and look of quiet but rather surprised attention—not specially reverent, but looking keenly out from under her eyelids, like a careful servant receiving an order?

Well—those are all Giovanni's own notions;—not the least classical, nor scientific, nor even like a pretty, sentimental modern woman. Like a Florentine woman—in Giovanni's time—it may be; at all events, very certainly, what Giovanni thought proper to carve.

Now examine your modern edition. An entirely proper Greco-Roman academy plaster bust, with a proper nose, and proper mouth, and a round chin, and an expression of the most solemn reverence; always, of course, of a classical description. Very fine, perhaps. But not Giovanni.

After Eve's head, let us look at her feet. Giovanni has his own positive notions about those also. Thin and bony, to excess, the right, undercut all along, so that the profile looks as thin as the mere elongated line on an Etruscan vase; and the right showing the five toes all well separate, nearly straight, and the larger ones almost as long as fingers! the shin bone above carried up in as severe and sharp a curve as the edge of a sword.

Now examine the modern copy. Beautiful little fleshy, Venus-de'-Medici feet and toes—no undercutting to the right foot,—the left having the great-toe properly laid over the second, according to the ordinances of schools and shoes, and a well-developed academic and operatic calf and leg. Again charming, of course. But only according to Mr. Gibson or Mr. Power—not according to Giovanni.

Farther, and finally, note the delight with which Giovanni has dwelt, though without exaggeration, on the muscles of the breast and ribs in the Adam; while he has subdued all away into virginal severity in Eve. And then note, and with conclusive admiration, how in the exact and only place where the poor modern fool's anatomical knowledge should have been shown, the wretch loses his hold of it! How he has entirely missed and effaced the grand Greek pectoral muscles of Giovanni's Adam, but has studiously added what mean fleshliness he could to the Eve; and marked with black spots the nipple and navel, where Giovanni left only the severe marble in pure light.

These instances are enough to enable you to detect the insolent changes in the design of Giovanni made by the modern Academy-student in so far as they relate to form absolute. I must farther, for a few moments, request your attention to the alterations made in the light and shade.

You may perhaps remember some of the passages. They occur frequently, both in my inaugural lectures, and in "Aratra Pentelici," in which I have pointed out the essential connection between the schools of sculpture and those of chiaroscuro. I have always spoken of the Greek, or essentially sculpture-loving schools, as chiaroscurist; always of the Gothic, or colour-loving schools, as non-chiaroscurist. And in one place, (I have not my books here, and cannot refer to it,) I have even defined sculpture as light-and-shade drawing with the chisel. Therefore, the next point you have to look to, after the absolute characters of form, is the mode in which the sculptor has placed his shadows, both to express these, and to force the eye to the points of his composition which he wants looked at. You cannot possibly see a more instructive piece of work, in these respects, than Giovanni's design of the

Nativity, Plate X. So far as I yet know Christian art, this is the central type of the treatment of the subject; it has all the intensity and passion of the earliest schools, together with a grace of repose which even in Ghiberti's beautiful Nativity, founded upon it, has scarcely been increased, but rather lost in languor. The motive of the design is the frequent one among all the early masters; the Madonna lifts the covering from the cradle to show the Child to one of the servants, who starts forward adoring. All the light and shade is disposed

{*Illustration: PLATE XII.—THE ANNUNCIATION AND VISITATION.*}

to fix the eye on these main actions. First, one intense deeply-cut mass of shadow, under the pointed arch, to throw out the head and lifted hand of the Virgin. A vulgar sculptor would have cut all black behind the head; Giovanni begins with full shadow; then subdues it with drapery absolutely quiet in fall; then lays his fullest possible light on the head, the hand, and the edge of the lifted veil.

He has undercut his Madonna's profile, being his main aim, too delicately for time to spare; happily the deep-cut brow is left, and the exquisitely refined line above, of the veil and hair. The rest of the work is uninjured, and the sharpest edges of light are still secure. You may note how the passionate action of the servant is given by the deep shadows under and above her arm, relieving its curves in all their length, and by the recess of shade under the cheek and chin, which lifts the face.

Now take your modern student's copy, and look how *he* has placed his lights and shades. You see, they go as nearly as possible exactly where Giovanni's *don't*. First, pure white under this Gothic arch, where Giovanni has put his fullest dark. Secondly, just where Giovanni has used his whole art of chiselling, to soften his stone away, and show the wreaths of the Madonna's hair lifting her veil behind, the accursed modern blockhead carves his shadow straight down, because he thinks that will be more in the style of Michael Angelo. Then he takes the shadows away from behind the profile, and from under the chin, and from under the arm, and puts in two grand square blocks of dark at the ends of the cradle, that you may be safe to look at that, instead of the Child. Next, he takes it all away from under the servant's arms, and lays it all behind above the calf of her leg. Then, not having wit enough to notice Giovanni's undulating surface beneath the drapery of the bed on the left, he limits it with a hard parallel-sided bar of shade, and insists on the vertical fold under the Madonna's arm, which Giovanni has purposely cut flat that it may not interfere with the arm above; finally, the modern animal has missed the only pieces of womanly form which Giovanni admitted, the rounded right arm and softly revealed breast; and absolutely removed, as if it were no part of the composition, the horizontal incision at the base of all—out of which the first folds of the drapery rise.

I cannot give you any better example, than this modern Academy-work, of the total ignorance of the very first meaning of the word 'Sculpture' into which the popular schools of existing art are plunged. I will not insist, now, on the uselessness, or worse, of their endeavours to represent the older art, and of the necessary futility of their judgment of it. The conclusions to which I wish to lead you on these points will be the subject of future lectures, being of too great importance for examination here. But you cannot spend your time in more profitable study than by examining and comparing, touch for touch, the treatment of light and shadow in the figures of the Christ and sequent angels, in Plates VIII. and IX., as we have partly examined those of the subject before us; and in thus assuring yourself of the uselessness of trusting to any ordinary modern copyists, for anything more than the rudest chart or map—and even that inaccurately surveyed—of ancient design.

The last plate given in this volume contains the two lovely subjects of the Annunciation and Visitation, which, being higher from the ground, are better preserved than the groups represented in the other plates. They will be found to justify, in subtlety of chiselling, the title I gave to Giovanni, of the Canova of the thirteenth century.

I am obliged to leave without notice, at present, the branch of ivy, given in illustration of the term 'marble rampant,' at the base of Plate VIII. The foliage of Orvieto can only be rightly described in connection with the great scheme of leaf-ornamentation which ascended from the ivy of the Homeric period in the sculptures of Cyprus, to the roses of Botticelli, and laurels of Bellini and Titian.

Milton Keynes UK
Ingram Content Group UK Ltd.
UKHW030742071024
449371UK00006B/635